Prevention's

FIT AND FAST MEALS
IN MINUTES

OVER 175 DELICIOUS, HEALTHY RECIPES
IN 30 MINUTES OR LESS

Prevention's

FIT AND FAST MEALS
IN MINUTES

LINDA GASSENHEIMER

author of the best-selling Low-Carb Meals in Minutes
and winner of the James Beard Award

RODALE

© 2006 by Linda Gassenheimer

All rights reserved. No part of this publication may be reproduced or transmitted in any form or by any means,
electronic or mechanical, including photocopying, recording, or any other information storage and retrieval
system, without the written permission of the publisher.

Printed in the United States of America
Rodale Inc. makes every effort to use acid-free ♾, recycled paper ♻.

Photographs by Mitch Mandel
Book design by Christina Gaugler
Cover photograph: Catalonian Paella (Fideua), page 207

Library of Congress Cataloging-in-Publication Data

Gassenheimer, Linda.
    Prevention's fit and fast meals in minutes : over 175 delicious, healthy recipes in 30 minutes or less / by Linda
Gassenheimer.
        p.   cm.
    Includes index.
    ISBN-13 978–1–59486–416–2   hardcover
    ISBN-10 1–59486–416–0   hardcover
    ISBN-13 978–1–59486–417–9   paperback
    ISBN-10 1–59486–417–9   paperback
    1. Quick and easy cookery.   2. Cookery, International.   I. Prevention (Emmaus, Pa.)   II. Title.
11I. Title: Fit and fast meals in minutes.
TX833.5.G38   2006
641.5′55—dc22   2006014410

Distributed to the book trade by Holtzbrinck Publishers

2   4   6   8   10   9   7   5   3   hardcover
2   4   6   8   10   9   7   5   3   paperback

To my husband, Harold, for his support, enthusiasm and love

CONTENTS

LUNCH

DINNER

DESSERTS

ENTERTAINING

Acknowledgments

Many thanks and much love go to my husband, Harold. This book could not have been written without his patience and help. He encouraged and assisted me from advice on creating the recipes to tasting and testing them.

Shea Zukowski, my editor at Rodale, has been a delight to work with and a much valued colleague. Many thanks, Shea.

Lisa Ekus has been my trusted friend for many years and as my agent was a wonderful help in bringing this book to publication. Lisa, great working with you.

I'd also like to thank my family who have always supported my projects and encouraged me every step of the way: My son James, his wife, Patty, and their children, Zachary, Jacob, and Haley, who helped taste these recipes; my son John, his wife, Jill, and their children, Jeffrey and Joanna, who cheered me on; my son Charles, his wife, Lori and their son, Daniel, for their guidance; and my sister Roberta and brother-in-law Robert who provide and continuous sounding board for my ideas.

Thanks go to Kathy Martin, my editor at the Miami Herald, who has been a friend and booster for my columns and books.

Thank you to Joseph Cooper, radio host for WLRN National Public Radio, who has helped and encouraged me with my Food News & Views segment.

I'd like to thank the many readers who correspond with me from all over the US to say how much they enjoy my recipes. This kind of encouragement makes the solitary time in front of the computer worthwhile. You can continue to contact me through my Web site www.DinnerinMinutes.com.

Most important, I'd like to thank all of you who read this book and prepare the meals. I hope you enjoy them and reap the benefits as much as I've enjoyed creating the recipes and watching the wonderful results.

Prevention's

FIT AND FAST MEALS
IN MINUTES

INTRODUCTION

What should I do if I want to improve my diet?"

"How can I fit making dinner into my time-starved day?"

"Is there an easier way to make great food that's good for me too?"

These are the types of questions I'm most often asked by people who read my newspaper column and listen to my radio show.

Some experts appear to have the answers already. When unveiling the government's new Food Pyramid guidelines, Tommy Thompson, Health and Human Services secretary, said, "Do you want to look better? Do you want to feel better? You lower your calorie intake, you lower your carbs, your fats. You eat more fruits and vegetables, and you exercise. That's as simple as it can be."

But is it really that simple?

We all need quick, easy solutions to help us eat well every day. Most important, we need meals that our families will eat. But in my experience, most people discover the path that works best for them is trickier to follow than it looks.

In part, I think that's because it's a challenge to translate all the advice from the experts into practical, everyday menus. For many years, in fact, I worked with a group of doctors who hired me to do just that. They advised people to eat lean proteins, use monounsaturated fats, and lower their intake of processed foods and simple carbohydrates. And when clients inevitably asked, "So, what do we eat?" they called on me.

Recently, two very accomplished, professional women came up to me at a conference and said, "We get home late, we want to make a healthful dinner, but we don't know what to make and what to make in minutes. HELP!"

Clearly, I assured them, they were not alone in their desperation. I get questions just like theirs every day. And I've written this book to provide some answers because I've found that it's quite possible to enjoy healthy and delicious homemade food—even if you have little time to cook. You just need to have a plan.

MAKING NUTRITION A REALITY

In a nutshell, you'll find enough recipes in this book to cover 4 weeks of meals, including breakfast, lunch, and dinner; a dessert chapter; and a section with menus for entertaining friends. Within minutes, you can make fresh, appealing meals for two following these menus. Plus, the recipes double easily if you're cooking for more people.

When you're asked, "What's for dinner?" you can choose menus from around the world. Do you feel like Tex-Mex? Try the Mexican Pork and Bean Chili or Shrimp Quesadillas with Chipotle Corn Salad. Do you want a comforting down-home dinner? Turkey Skillet Casserole or Southwestern Chicken Burgers with Quick Slaw can fill the bill. For some ethnic flavors, there's Curry-Kissed Chicken with Carrots and Rice, Chinese Pork in Lettuce Puffs with Brown Rice and Peas, or Greek Lemon Fish with Cracked Wheat Salad. Have great food without breaking the calorie bank on the weekend with Walnut-Crusted Steak with Fennel and Bean Salad or Rosemary-Garlic Lamb Steak with Italian Tomatoes and Beans. And don't skip dessert. Velvety Chocolate Mousse or Very Berry Crepes are two of the tempting recipes. Having friends for dinner is a breeze with the chapter on entertaining. Casual Supper for Six, Barbecue Buffet, or Dinner Party for Six, for example, are menus that can be made without spending days in the kitchen. There are nine weekend menus in all.

The inspiration for many of these dishes comes from my travels around the world. I love going to open markets, seeing the local ingredients, and asking locals how they use them. As a trained chef with years of experience writing a syndicated column, "Dinner in Minutes," I have developed plenty of quick and easy techniques that let you enjoy these varied menus with little effort.

These are no-brainer meals. My "in minutes" approach covers all aspects of food, from purchasing to preparing ingredients to presenting delicious, complete meals. No need to think about how to cook a dish or what goes with it. Just use the recipes and enjoy good food.

Plus, when you follow the menu plan—including breakfast, lunch, dinner, and a dessert with dinner—you will be consuming an average of 1,400 calories per day, with 26 percent of calories from fat (of which 6 percent are from saturated fat), 29 percent of calories from protein, and 39 percent of calories from carbohydrates. In addition, the average daily fiber intake is over 27 grams, in line with the recommended daily requirement. When I give cooking demonstrations, people are surprised at how much food they can enjoy while still staying within these guidelines. Here are some of the other benefits you'll find:

Save Time in the Supermarket with

Organized Shopping Lists: Supermarkets have been supersized. Forgetting something in the dairy department when you're in the produce department can mean extra time navigating busy aisles to complete your list. The detailed shopping lists given with each menu note the ingredients according to the store departments.

One-Stop Shopping: No need to go to several stores for specialty items. All of the ingredients can be bought in a local supermarket. The helpful hints with each recipe give suggestions for substitutions if an ingredient is not available that day.

Buy Food That Helps You Assemble Meals in Minutes: Take advantage of what the supermarkets have to offer. Today, they sell many products that are not highly processed and are based on natural, wholesome ingredients. I've used these ingredients to assemble quick dinners.

Staples List: The staples list helps you plan your pantry. You will already have many of the ingredients for the recipes and only need to buy a few fresh items to make a meal.

Countdown: In addition to the helpful hints, each menu has a countdown so you can get the whole meal on the table at the same time. You can hit the kitchen on the run without having to plan or think about each step.

TOOLS FOR A HEALTHFUL
AND DELICIOUS LIFESTYLE

There's a reason why nutrition headlines are so attention grabbing. Who doesn't want to lower their risk of disease so they can live better—and quite possibly longer? There are a lot of things to enjoy in life, and I for one count eating well among them. In the most basic sense, a healthful diet means you're getting the right balance of nutrients, vitamins, and minerals in beneficial amounts.

Unfortunately, many popular diets take a "you can't have that" approach and would have us instead focus most of our attention on minimizing certain types of foods, and in some cases eliminating entire food groups altogether. The problem with this strategy is that by cutting out one particular part of your diet, other ingredients tend to be increased.

Low-fat diets, for example, led people to increase their carbohydrate intake. Remember the low-fat cookie craze? The popular logic was that if there's no fat in that little treat, it's okay to eat all you want. And who could eat only one cookie? Supermarkets couldn't keep these cookies on the shelves when they were introduced, and many people eating them gained weight. In retrospect, many experts agree that it was wrong to classify all fats as "bad." Monounsaturated fats, we now know, are essential to good health.

Similarly, the extreme low-carb diets that sanctioned any type of fat—including large amounts of saturated fat—helped people to lose weight, but many doctors reported their patients were landing in the hospital with intestinal problems due to the lack of fiber. In addition, cardiologists were concerned by the large amounts of protein that were consumed along with saturated fat, as well as the fact that most people gained their weight right back once they reintroduced carbohydrates into their diet. Many, it seemed, couldn't stay on this restrictive diet indefinitely. The media and manufacturers who jumped on the bandwagon helped lead people astray. A no-carb brownie with 450 calories eaten as a snack has very little nutrition and adds pounds rather than subtracting them. Again, it was wrong to classify all carbohydrates as "bad." Complex carbohydrates—those from fruits, vegetables, and whole grains—are important to a healthy diet, too.

Fortunately, the meals in this book don't force you into these types of choices. Instead, they include just the right balance of complex carbohydrates, monounsaturated fats, and lean proteins. Plus, the meal plans in this book are designed to make sure you get all the fruit and vegetable servings that you should. All of these factors play an important role in total health. Best of all, these remarkably easy recipes allow you to taste foods from around the world. And if you follow the 4-week plan, there's no need to count calories, fat, carbs, or protein. Just follow the meals and enjoy.

The Food-Health Connection

Of all that we know about how food affects our health, it's clear that eating to reach and maintain a healthy weight is a fundamental part of the equation. Just reducing your body weight by 10 percent will improve your blood chemistry. And according to the federal government, reaching your ideal weight may reduce your risk of chronic diseases such as heart disease, diabetes, osteoporosis, and certain cancers, and increase your chances for a longer life.

The importance of maintaining a healthy weight is a message we would all do well to hear. The Centers for Disease Control has reported that obesity may overtake smoking as the number-one cause of preventable deaths in the United States. To complicate matters, many types of obesity-related diseases, particularly coronary heart disease (CHD) and diabetes, can go undiagnosed until a major health scare surfaces. Some experts estimate that close to one-third of the people in this country, for example, are living with diabetes and don't even know it.

Another condition, prediabetes, appears to be even more prevalent, affecting 40 percent of our nation. A person with prediabetes has blood glucose levels that are higher than normal, but not high enough for a diagnosis of diabetes. Some studies show that most people with prediabetes develop type 2 diabetes in 10 years.

So what's the good news here? Research from the American Diabetes Association indicates that for people who have prediabetes, losing weight, eating a balanced diet, and exercising can stop the progression to diabetes. The recipes in this book will help you follow these guidelines. Here's how:

Whole Grains

Whole grains have received so much attention recently, the term has almost become a marketing catchphrase to imply something is healthy. But it's easy to understand the hype when you stop to consider how nutritious they really are. In general, foods made from whole grains tend to be much better for your health than those made from refined grains, such as white rice or white bread, because the entire grain seed is used: the bran, the germ, and the endosperm. The bran and germ have a wide range of vitamins, minerals, and fiber. Plus, whole grains offer complex carbohydrates, which are digested slowly and can help avoid some of the problems associated with prediabetes, diabetes, and coronary heart disease.

One of the most common problems, insulin spikes, occurs when simple carbohydrates such as refined sugar are quickly digested, causing the body to release a rush of insulin into the bloodstream. Insulin works by helping cells receive the glucose they need for fuel, effectively helping to convert blood sugar into energy. However, problems can occur when the body produces too much insulin, which then lingers in the bloodstream. This excess insulin sends signals to the brain asking for food, a pattern that's widely known in its most simple terms as food cravings. Complex carbohydrates, such as those found in whole grains, are digested more slowly, thereby avoiding a spike of insulin production.

If you find yourself feeling hungry a few hours after eating a meal based on simple carbohydrates (a large plate of pasta with little else on the plate), there's a good chance you may be insulin resistant. One study funded by the USDA Agricultural Research Service showed that those who consumed at least three servings of whole grain foods per day were less likely to experience insulin resistance.

Similarly, results from the Nurses' Health Study have revealed links between whole-grain intake and reduced risk of CHD, probably because of the many nutrients found in whole grains, specifically vitamin E, vitamin B_6, and folate. Each of these vitamins has been associated with lower risk of CHD in other studies.

Whole grains are abundant in the 4-week meal plan in this book, adding variety, flavor, and texture to your meals (as well as a wealth of nutrients). Some examples of whole grains are brown rice and whole grain breads. When you're shopping, look for whole wheat on the food label, not just the words wheat or 100 percent wheat. Some breads labeled simply 12-, 9-, or 7-grain could have one-third the fiber of similarly labeled whole wheat breads.

Fiber

Fiber is important for our digestive system to work well. There are two types of fiber: soluble and insoluble. Soluble fibers are absorbed by the body. According to a study from Johns Hopkins University, soluble fiber may also help lower blood cholesterol, and insoluble fiber tends to speed up the passage of material through the digestive tract and reduces the risk of colon cancer, as well as diverticular disease. Thus, insoluble fiber, usually referred to as roughage, is not absorbed but rather passed through the body with certain digestive benefits. This type of fiber includes fruit and vegetable skins, as well as wheat bran and whole grain cereals.

Regardless of the type, fiber is essential to proper nutrition because it assists in digestion and promotes regularity in the body. In addition, fiber-rich foods tend to take more time to eat, so they fill the stomach more slowly and allow time for our brain to tell us we're full. The USDA daily fiber recommendation is between 25 and 30 grams a day. This is roughly the amount of fiber in three to five servings of fresh fruit and four servings of vegetables, plus whole grains and cereals. Sources of soluble fiber are citrus fruits, apples, carrots, potatoes, barley, oats, and dried peas and beans. Sources of insoluble fiber are wheat bran, whole grains, legumes, cabbage, beets, and cauliflower. The average American consumes only about 15 grams a day, roughly half of what's recommended. However, if you follow the meal plans in this book, you'll meet that recommended amount without a problem.

Antioxidants

One of the most serious problems about the typical modern diet is the lack of fruits and vegetables. When we rely so heavily on processed foods, we not only deprive ourselves of a fantastic array of textures and flavors, we also come up short on the antioxidants that we need for good health. In a nutshell, antioxidants are important nutrients that help the body fight the natural damage that occurs to all of us at a cellular level. Specifically, antioxidants work to neutralize harmful free radicals, the destructive compounds that damage the structure and function of the body's cells. According to the National Cancer Institute, the most common form of free radicals in humans is oxygen. When an oxygen molecule (O_2) becomes electrically charged or "radicalized," it tries to steal electrons from other molecules, causing damage to the DNA and other molecules. Over time, such damage may become irreversible and lead to a host of problems, including cancer and heart disease. Antioxidants are often described as "mopping up" free radicals, meaning they neutralize the electrical charge and prevent the free radicals from taking electrons from other molecules.

Moreover, for all the people who'd prefer to take a pill to prevent the problems associated with free radical damage, a number of health organizations, including the American Heart Association, recommend we get our antioxidants from food, not supplements. It seems research fails to justify routine use of antioxidant supplements to prevent or treat cardiovascular disease. Other bodies of research also make a case for why we should rely on antioxidants from food. Ongoing results from the Nurses' Health Study, for example, reveal that higher intakes of fruit and vegetables are associated with lower risk of heart disease. Following the meals in this book will provide ample amounts of foods containing antioxidants.

Antioxidants are abundant in fruits and vegetables, as well as in other foods including some meats, poultry, and fish. Here is a quick rundown of antioxidants and common foods containing them.

Beta-carotene is found in many foods that are orange in color, including sweet potatoes, carrots, cantaloupe, squash, apricots, pumpkin, and mangoes. Some leafy vegetables, including collard greens, spinach, and kale, are also rich in beta-carotene.

Lutein is best known for its association with healthy eyes and is abundant in green, leafy vegetables such as collard greens, spinach, and kale.

Lycopene is a potent antioxidant found in tomatoes, watermelon, guava, papaya, apricots, pink grapefruit, blood oranges, and other foods.

Selenium is a mineral, not an antioxidant nutrient. However, it is a component of antioxidant enzymes. Plant foods like rice and wheat are major dietary sources of selenium. Meats and bread are common sources of dietary selenium. Brazil nuts also contain large quantities of selenium.

Vitamin A is found in liver, sweet potatoes, carrots, milk, egg yolks, and broccoli.

Vitamin C, also known as ascorbic acid, can be found in high abundance in many fruits and vegetables and in cereals, beef, poultry, and fish. Oranges are a good source of vitamin C. A cup of broccoli has more vitamin C than a navel orange.

Vitamin E, also known as alpha-tocopherol, is found in almonds; in many oils including wheat germ, safflower, corn, and soybean; and in mangoes, nuts, and broccoli.

Vitamin B_6 can be found in cereal grains, carrots, peas, spinach, potatoes, milk, cheese, eggs, fish, and beef liver. A vitamin B_6 (pyridoxine) deficiency can affect nerves, skin, and mucous membranes.

Vitamin B_{12} helps maintain healthy nerve cells and red blood cells and is commonly found in a variety of foods such as fish, shellfish, meats, and dairy products. It is frequently used in combination with other B vitamins in a vitamin B formulation. The human body is able to store several years' worth of Vitamin B_{12}. However, the elderly are most at risk for B_{12} deficiency. Also, strict vegetarians and vegans need to make sure they are getting enough B_{12} in their food.

Folate and folic acid are forms of a water-soluble B vitamin. Folate occurs naturally in food, and folic acid is the synthetic form of this vitamin. It helps the body form red blood cells and aids in the formation of genetic material within every body cell. It is found in asparagus, mushrooms, tomatoes, and green leafy and cruciferous vegetables such as spinach and broccoli. It's also found in bananas, melons, lemons, beef liver, and legumes.

Fats

Here's a sobering nutrition fact: A gram of fat has more than twice as many calories as a gram of protein or carbohydrate. So in terms of weight loss, the importance of paying attention to the amount of fat in our diet is practically a no-brainer. However, recent studies have shed new light on our understanding of the impact different types of dietary fats can have on our health, especially in relation to the total fat we consume.

But first, let's start with a quick overview

of what we're up against. There are three basic types of dietary fat that have been discussed for decades. Monounsaturated and polyunsaturated fats are generally regarded as the "right fats" and are found in olive oil, canola oil, corn oil, or safflower oil. These fats are important for growth and development and should make up 20 to 35 percent of your diet. Saturated fat, which is found in animal products such as butter and red meat, is commonly associated with high cholesterol. The American Heart Association recommends getting no more (and preferably less) than 10 percent of our total calories from saturated fats.

A fourth type of fat, trans fats, has gained quite a bit of notoriety in the past few years, and with good reason. Trans fats result from the hydrogenation of oils, which turn them into a solid form. They're found in many processed foods, such as french fries, microwave oven popcorn, and margarine. These are considered artery-clogging fats.

Large population-based studies have shown that trans fats are associated with an even higher risk of heart disease than saturated fats. For this reason, many experts have recommended that foods with trans fats should be avoided. Although many manufacturers have reduced or eliminated the amount of trans fats in their products, the easiest way to avoid them is to focus on whole foods like the ones used in this book.

What's surprising is that going to extremes—either too much of the wrong fats in the diet or not enough of the right ones—seems to have an adverse impact on health. A large body of evidence has demonstrated the dangerous link between saturated fats and heart disease. However, results from studies at Penn State University have shown that higher-fat diets that are high in "good" fats and low in saturated fats can lower the total level of LDL cholesterol in the blood. On the other hand, a low intake of monounsaturated fats and oils (less than 20 percent of calories) raises the risk of not getting enough vitamin E and essential fatty acids. This may contribute to unfavorable changes in HDL (high-density lipoprotein) blood cholesterol and triglycerides.

The good news is there's no need to count your percent of calories with the recipes in this book. Just enjoy the meals and know that they follow these guidelines.

Proteins

Lean proteins are important for balanced eating. Proteins are slowly digested and, as a result, help to curb your appetite. They also act as building blocks for bones, muscles, skin, and blood. And they are important components of enzymes, hormones, and vitamins.

Skinless chicken parts and turkey breast are the leanest cuts of poultry. Fish is another good source. The leanest cuts of pork are pork tenderloin and pork loin. Round steaks, top loin, and top sirloin are some of the leanest cuts of beef. From the deli department, choose lean turkey, roast beef, or ham. Another good source of protein comes from legumes (kidney beans, black beans) and some vegetables such as avocado. Animal protein has saturated fat, but meat can still be enjoyed by choosing lean cuts and choosing the right cooking methods to minimize fat. You'll enjoy flavors from around the world using lean proteins in a variety of appetizing meals here.

WHAT WE SHOULD EAT

As I stressed earlier, it's one thing to know in general terms what types of foods you should eat. It's an entirely different situation to try to navigate all of the choices that present themselves in a modern grocery store. Here then is a practical guide to the types of foods you should place in your grocery cart as frequently as possible:

Whole Grains

Bran cereals (look for about 13 grams per ⅓ to ½ cup serving, such as Fiber One or All Bran Bran Buds)
Brown rice
Cracked wheat (bulgur)
Oats
Quinoa
Whole grain breads (whole wheat, rye, multigrains)
Whole wheat pastas
Whole wheat tortillas
Wild rice

Good Fats

Avocado oil
Canola oil
Nut oils
Olive oil

Vegetables

Vegetables are an important source of fiber, vitamins, minerals, and cancer-fighting phytochemicals, and are low in calories. Each vegetable has its own important vitamins and minerals. Throughout these menus, you will be eating a variety of vegetables to ensure you are benefiting from all of their properties.

Asparagus
Avocado
Bean sprouts
Beets
Broccoli
Cabbage
Carrots
Cauliflower
Celery
Cucumber
Dark green leafy vegetables
Garlic
Green beans
Green, red, yellow bell peppers
Mesclun
Mushrooms
Okra
Onions
Peas
Romaine lettuce
Shallots
Snow peas
Spinach
Sugar snap peas
Sweet potatoes
Tomatoes
Watercress
Zucchini

Dry Beans and Peas

Beans have been called the near-perfect food. They are slowly digested, are high in complex carbohydrates, are a nonmeat protein, are a good source of fiber, and are full of vitamins and minerals. All beans have a good amount of B vitamins and are rich in iron, calcium, zinc, and potassium.

Black beans
Chickpeas
Kidney beans
Lentils
Navy beans
Soy beans
White beans

Fruit

Apples
Apricots
Bananas
Blackberries
Blueberries
Cantaloupe
Cherries
Grapefruit
Honeydew
Kiwis
Lemons
Limes
Mangoes
Oranges
Peaches
Pears
Pineapples
Plums
Raspberries
Strawberries
Tangerines

Lean Poultry and Meat

Chicken (with skin removed)
Pork tenderloin and pork loin
Round steak
Top sirloin steak
Turkey
Veal

Seafood

Fatty fish—such as salmon, herring, or mackerel—that contain omega-3 fatty acids
Fin fish, such as snapper, tilapia, grouper, sole, mahi mahi, or cod
Shellfish

Deli

Ask for lean or lower-fat meats (and watch labels for lower-sodium brands, too)
Chicken breast
Ham
Roast beef
Turkey

Dairy

Eggs
Reduced-fat cheese
Skim milk
Yogurt (low-fat or nonfat)

HELPFUL HINTS
AND COOKING TIPS

In my experience, using the fastest cooking methods is only half the battle to great, quick meals. Knowing which ingredients to use—and how to buy them—can save you invaluable time before you even step foot in the kitchen. In addition to the helpful hints I provide with each menu, keep the following advice in mind to save even more time shopping and cooking:

Parmesan Cheese Using the best quality cheese means you can get more flavor satisfaction while eating a smaller quantity. Buy good quality Parmigiano-Reggiano cheese and chop or grate it in the food processor. Freeze extra for quick use. You can quickly spoon out what you need and leave the rest frozen.

To shave or make Parmesan curls, bring a block of cheese to room temperature and use a potato peeler to make thin strips.

Buying Shrimp Most shrimp sold in the United States comes to the market frozen. Instead of buying the defrosted shrimp from the seafood case, ask for shrimp that is still frozen and keep some on hand at home for quick meals. You can buy raw or cooked, peeled shrimp.

To defrost the shrimp quickly, place it in a bowl in the sink and run cold water into it. They will be ready in less than 5 minutes.

Pasteurized Egg Whites Pasteurized liquid egg whites can be used when egg whites are called for in a recipe. Follow the equivalents on the carton. They are used in many recipes in this book, but cannot be used if egg whites need to be whipped.

Produce Department Shredded carrots, sliced celery, diced peppers, chopped onions, and trimmed green beans are a few of the convenience items available in the produce department. Watch for other items that will save you preparation time in the kitchen.

Salad bars are another place to buy prepared vegetables.

Using Wine and Spirits If you do not have the wine or spirit called for in a recipe and do not want to buy a whole bottle, splits or small bottles can be found in most liquor stores.

Chopping and Slicing Herbs and Spices A quick way to chop fresh basil, chives, cilantro, parsley, mint, or rosemary is to snip the leaves off the stems with a scissors.

A quick way to slice scallions is to cut them with a scissors.

Stir-frying For easy stir-frying, place all of the prepared ingredients on a cutting board or plate in order of use. You won't have to look at the recipe once you start to cook.

Make sure the wok or skillet is very hot before adding the ingredients. The oil should be smoking.

Once the ingredients have been added to the wok, let them sit a minute without tossing them. This gives the wok a chance to regain heat lost when the cold ingredients were added.

Using an Electric Stove Top For quick high-heat/low-heat action, heat two burners, one on high and the other on low. Move the pot back and forth between them as necessary.

Egg Whites Bring egg whites to room temperature for best whipping results. If the eggs are cold and you want to use them right away, place them in a bowl of warm water for a few minutes.

Whipped egg whites become soft when sugar is added. Sugar is usually added once the whites are stiff. Work quickly when the sugar is added and continue to whip the whites until stiff again.

Washing Herbs A quick way to wash watercress, parsley, arugula, or basil is to place the bunch head first in a bowl of water. Leave them there for a minute and lift them out by their stems. Shake them dry. The dirt and sand will be left in the bowl.

Microwave Cooking Several recipes give the method for using a microwave oven. Timing can vary, depending on the power of each microwave oven. Test the timing given in the recipe, and then alter accordingly.

Be careful when using a microwave oven. Food continues to cook for a few minutes after it is removed from a microwave oven and can easily be overcooked.

Cooking Seafood Heat a baking tray under the broiler before adding the fish fillets. This creates bottom heat and means you don't have to turn the fish during cooking.

The general rule is to cook fish 10 minutes per inch of thickness. If your fillet is thicker, add a minute; if it is thinner, subtract a minute. However, since fish continues to cook when it is removed from the heat, make sure to cook the fish 8 minutes per inch if you are concerned about overcooking.

To check that the fish is ready, pull some of the flesh away with the point of a knife. It should be opaque not translucent.

STAPLES

Keep these staples on hand and you will only have to pick up a few fresh items to make these dinners. Many of my readers tell me that this staples list helps them organize their pantry. They don't have a lot of ingredients that are never used or used only once.

Sauces, Dressings

Dijon mustard
Hot-pepper sauce
Mayonnaise
Olive oil and vinegar dressing
Reduced-fat mayonnaise
Reduced-fat oil and vinegar dressing

Dairy

Eggs
Skim milk

Dry Goods

All-purpose flour
Brown sugar
Coffee
Cornstarch
High-fiber bran cereal
Sugar
Sugar substitute
10-minute brown rice

Canned or Bottle Goods

Canned black beans, canellini (white
    kidney) beans, red kidney beans
Fat-free, low-sodium chicken broth
Honey

Low-fat, low-sodium pasta sauce
Orange juice
Tomato salsa

Oils and Vinegars

Apple cider vinegar
Balsamic vinegar
Canola oil
Olive oil
Olive oil spray
Sesame oil
Vegetable oil spray
White vinegar

Spices, Herbs, and Seasonings

Black peppercorns
Ground cinnamon
Ground nutmeg
Ground oregano
Salt
Vanilla extract

Frozen

Frozen chopped or diced green bell
    pepper
Frozen chopped or diced onion

Breads

Rye bread
Whole grain bread
Whole wheat bread

Produce

Garlic
Onion
Red onion

EQUIPMENT

These meals can be made without a lot of specialty equipment. Here's a list of items that will help get these meals on the table in minutes.

Food Processor Slicing and chopping can be done quickly with a food processor or a mini-chopper.

Garlic Press There are many varieties of garlic presses on the market. I prefer the ones that allow you to crush the garlic without peeling the skin away.

Grater A simple grater that has one side for fine grating and one for shredding is very useful. I use it for cheese and to prepare fresh ginger.

Knives Three different knife sizes are all you need for most cutting and slicing—a 4-inch paring knife, an 8-inch chef's knife, and a small serrated stainless steel knife for fruit and tomatoes.

Knife Sharpener A dull knife can be dangerous in the kitchen. It can slip or slide across the ingredient you are cutting. An electric or hand knife sharpener will help to keep your knives ready for use.

Meat Thermometer Chefs say they can tell when meat is ready by touching it. I find a good meat thermometer much easier and more accurate. An instant-read thermometer or one with a probe that goes into the meat and has a cord that is connected to the dial lets you read the temperature easily. It can be used for meats in the oven, on the stove, or on the grill.

Microwave Oven Several recipes use this fast-cooking appliance. Another plus in using a microwave oven is that all of the cooking dishes go into the dishwasher.

Skillets and Saucepans You only need a few skillets and saucepans to make most of these recipes—a standard nonstick skillet (9 to 10 inches) with a lid, a small nonstick skillet (7 inches), a large (3- to 4-quart) saucepan with a lid, and a wok.

Scale Although equivalent cup measurements are given where weights are listed, I recommend using a small kitchen scale. It will help you measure ingredients quickly and accurately.

Vegetable Peeler Like a knife, a vegetable peeler needs to be very sharp. It should be replaced often to make peeling easier.

MAKING THE RIGHT CHOICES

Portion distortion is a term used to describe a condition we've all experienced. According to numerous studies, portion sizes in the marketplace, from restaurants to grocery stores, are way out of control. Researchers at New York University compared serving sizes of foods in the most popular take-out establishments, fast-food outlets, and family-type restaurants against the U.S. Department of Agriculture Food Guide Pyramid. Here are some surprising results:

- Cookies were seven times the standard portion sizes.
- Cooked pasta was often nearly five times the standard portion sizes.
- Muffins weighed over three times the standard portion sizes.

Another study found that the American croissant is bigger and contains more calories than one in France. When the bagel was introduced to the United States, it weighed 1½ ounces and contained 116 calories. Today's bagels weigh about 4 to 4½ ounces and may contain over 300 calories.

To practice better portion control when you're eating at home:

Use smaller plates.

Choose proportionate servings. Fill half your plate with vegetables, a fourth with protein, and a fourth with a starch, such as rice.

Focus on your food. Sit and relax at mealtime. Don't eat in front of the TV or computer.

Reduce soft-drink consumption. These add unnecessary calories, mostly simple carbohydrates, so drink at least eight 8-ounce glasses of water a day.

SIZING IT UP

Following the recipes in this book will give you an idea of the portion sizes and the types of foods you should be eating. Use the following chart to know at a glance how certain ingredients measure, to give an approximate value.

To estimate your portion	Make sure it's about this size
3 to 4 ounces meat or fish	a pack of tissues or deck of cards
6 ounces meat or fish	a checkbook
1 ounce nuts	2 shot glasses
1 ounce cheese	2 dominoes or your thumb
1 cup cooked rice or pasta	the size of your fist
¾ cup frozen yogurt or ice cream	1 tennis ball
Tortilla	a small plate, about 7 inches
Muffin	a large egg

GENERAL EATING-OUT TIPS

With many of our meals eaten out, it's hard to maintain a healthful lifestyle. Here are some other general eating-out tips that can help.

Have a snack beforehand. It may seem counterintuitive to have a small snack before going out to eat—after all, you may be going to a restaurant because you want to spend a night out of the kitchen or your cupboard is bare. However, going to a restaurant on an empty stomach is a recipe for disaster. Eat a small piece of low-fat cheese or a few whole wheat crackers before heading out the door, and you'll find it's far easier to make wise choices once you're looking at a big menu.

Don't go out for drinks on an empty stomach. Drinks are called aperitifs because they increase your appetite. One drink will make you hungry, and you will probably eat the first thing that you see. Also, if it's going to be a long cocktail hour, start with sparkling water or a diet drink before ordering a glass of wine or a drink.

Delay the bread. There's nothing wrong with enjoying the bread basket—the problem is that it's so hard to resist eating all of it at once. Ask for the bread basket to be brought to the table with the main course. This will keep you from nibbling while you wait for your order.

Order wisely. Instead of an appetizer and main course, opt for smaller portions by ordering two appetizers instead. Plan to share an entrée with your dining companion. Likewise, order one dessert and share it with the table. And when at fast-food restaurants, opt for the salads or grilled meat or fish.

Ask for salad dressing on the side. Dip the salad into the dressing or spoon a tablespoon of it over the salad.

Start with a doggie bag. Often restaurant portions are so huge, it's easy to feel satisfied even if you only eat half of what is served. Ask for the doggie bag to arrive when your dinner is served so you can set some of your meal aside.

SHOPPING GUIDELINES

The markets today are filled with products that can help us get a meal on the table in minutes. There are many brands to choose from. Here is a chart to help you when reading the labels to select the ones that fit our nutritional guidelines. Once you've found the products you like, keep them on hand for quick cooking.

Read the nutrition label carefully to be sure of the quantity for which the information is given.

	Calories	Carbohydrates	Fat	Sodium	Fiber
Oil and vinegar dressing (1 tablespoon)	75	0.5–1.5 g	8 g	0 mg	
Low-fat oil and vinegar dressing (1 tablespoon)	26	1.2 g	2.2 g	114 mg	
Mayonnaise made from soybean, canola, or olive oil (1 tablespoon)	100	0.4 g	11 g	4 mg	
Reduced-fat mayonnaise (1 tablespoon)	50	1.3 g	4.9 g	120 mg	
Tomato sauce, low sodium (1 tablespoon)	60–80	12 g	0 g	40 mg	
Pasta sauce, low sodium (1 cup)	120	26 g	0 g	740 mg	
Nonfat, low-sodium chicken broth (1 cup)	15	1 g	0 g	570 mg	
High-fiber bran cereals (½ cup)	60	24 g	2.2 g	270 mg	13 g
Lean ham and Canadian bacon (1 ounce)	41	0.4 g	1.6 g	341 mg	
Reduced-fat cheese (1 ounce)	49	0.5 g	2.0 g	174 mg	
Low-fat frozen yogurt (½ cup)	100	18.3 g	4.5 g	75 mg	
Whole wheat bread (1 ounce, about 1 slice)	40	10 g	1 g	4 g	5 g

FOUR-WEEK MENU CHART

Fit and Fast Meals in Minutes—Week 1

	Breakfast	Lunch	Dinner
Sunday	Banana-Apricot Egg Crepes p. 28	Ham, Pepper, and Onion Pizza p. 96	Mushroom Pesto Steak and Hot Pepper Potatoes p. 178
Monday	Granola Yogurt Parfait and Cheddar Eggs p. 38	Smoked Trout Salad and Pineapple and Coconut Flakes p. 114	Poached Chicken with Fresh Tomato-Mayonnaise Sauce and Rice Salad p. 164
Tuesday	Microwave Salsa Scramble and Oatmeal p. 43	Roasted Chicken and Cheese Panini and Pineapples and Honey p. 106	Halibut in Cider and Saffron Rice p. 138
Wednesday	Breakfast Burrito and Bran Cereal p. 30	Ham, Melon, and Endive Salad p. 94	Turkey Skillet Casserole and Tossed Salad p. 168
Thursday	Ham and Apple Butter Omelet and Banana Bran Cereal p. 39	Black Bean, Couscous, and Pepper Salad p. 76	Portobello Parmesan over Linguine p. 180
Friday	Strawberry-Peach Smoothie and Roast Beef Wrap p. 48	Waldorf Wrap p. 124	Cajun-Bronzed Mahi Mahi and Rice and Spinach Pilaf p. 130
Saturday	Honey-Walnut French Toast p. 41	Lemon-Pepper Shrimp Salad p. 98	Southwestern Chicken Burgers and Quick Slaw p. 160

Fit and Fast Meals in Minutes—Week 2

	Breakfast	Lunch	Dinner
Sunday	Smoked Trout Bagel p. 46	Ham and Wild Mushroom Quiche p. 92	Walnut-Crusted Steak and Fennel Bean Salad p. 188
Monday	Poached Pesto Eggs and Bran Cereal p. 45	Shrimp and Peach Pasta Salad p. 112	Crispy Chicken and Provencal Vegetables (Ratatouille) p. 154
Tuesday	Apple-Cinnamon Oatmeal and Turkey Cheese Wrap p. 26	Middle Eastern Plate p. 100	Catfish with Mango Chutney and Black Bean and Rice Salad p. 132
Wednesday	Microwave Spinach and Cheese Scramble and Oatmeal p. 44	Ham and Gorgonzola Wrap p. 90	Italian Meat Loaf and Hot Pepper Lentils p. 158
Thursday	Ginger Oatmeal p. 36	Po' Boy Sandwich p. 104	Shrimp Quesadilla and Chipotle Corn Salad p. 144
Friday	Soft-Cooked Eggs and Bran Cereal p. 47	Creamy Lettuce Soup and Mixed Melon Salad p. 82	Julia's Simple Salmon and Gratineed Cauliflower p. 140
Saturday	Hot and Sweet Pepper Rolls p. 42	Texas Tuna Burger with Jalapeño Mayonnaise and Banana and Strawberries p. 118	Brazilian-Style Chicken with Quinoa p. 150

Fit and Fast Meals in Minutes—Week 3

	Breakfast	Lunch	Dinner
Sunday	Fresh Herb and Ham Frittata p. 34	Seafood Antipasto Plate (Antipasto di Mare) p. 110	Rosemary-Garlic Lamb Steak and Italian Tomatoes and Beans p. 182
Monday	Cocoa Espresso Smoothie and Cheddar-Ham Melt p. 32	Frisee, Pear, and Roquefort Salad p. 88	Curry-Kissed Chicken and Carrots and Rice p. 156
Tuesday	Sunnyside-Up Canadian Bacon and Cheese Toast and Bran Cereal p. 66	Turkey Cranberry Wrap p. 120	Greek Lemon Fish and Cracked Wheat Salad (Tabbouleh) p. 136
Wednesday	Good Morning Shake and Melted Cheese Toasts p. 37	Goulash Soup and Cinnamon Grapefruit p. 86	Mexican Pork and Bean Chili and Shredded Lettuce Salad p. 176
Thursday	Tex-Mex Eggs and Tortilla Chips (Migas) and Bran Cereal p. 31	Club Sandwich Wrap p. 78	Sicilian Swordfish with Broccoli Linguine p. 146
Friday	Fruited Cottage Cheese p. 35	Crab Salad Melt p. 80	Jacques Pépin's Mediterranean Chicken over Spinach and Garlic Beans p. 160
Saturday	Crispy Chinese Pancakes p. 33	Barbecued Chicken Sandwich p. 74	Chinese Pork in Lettuce Puffs and Brown Rice and Peas p. 174

Fit and Fast Meals in Minutes—Week 4

	Breakfast	Lunch	Dinner
Sunday	Wild Turkey Hash p. 69	Tuscan Tomato and Bread Salad and Orange and Pine Nut Slices p. 122	Veal Roquefort with Linguine and French Green Beans p. 186
Monday	Sun-Dried Tomato and Basil Scramble and Raspberry Bran Cereal p. 65	Spicy Asian Shrimp Salad p. 116	Mexican Orange Chicken and Green Pepper Rice p. 162
Tuesday	Banana Yogurt–Bran Cup and Roast Beef Open-Faced Sandwich p. 27	Sausage and Beet Salad p. 108	Crab Scampi and Spaghetti p. 134
Wednesday	Wild Mushroom Parmesan Omelet and Strawberry Bran Cereal p. 68	Pan Bagnat p. 102	Wasabi Chicken and Pan-Roasted Corn and Broccoli p. 170
Thursday	Turkey Pastrami on Rye p. 67	Curried Egg Salad Sandwich p. 84	Salmon Gazpacho and Rice Salad p. 142
Friday	Herbed Goat Cheese and Chive Scramble and Blueberry Bran Cereal p. 40	Greek Bean and Vegetable Soup (Fassoulada) p. 89	Stir-Fried Diced Pork and Chinese Noodles p. 184
Saturday	Blueberry Pancakes p. 29	Asian-Mexican Tostados p. 72	Chicken Satay with Thai Peanut Sauce and Broccoli and Rice p. 152

BREAKFAST

Many of us eat breakfast on the run or don't eat it at all. The question I get most often from those who want to balance their day with healthful meals is how can I fit breakfast into my schedule. I have kids to get to school, or I have an early meeting or need to be at my desk very early in the morning. And those who take the time for breakfast ask me what can they have besides coffee and a muffin or bagel. It is important to start your day off with breakfast. Achieving nutritional balance needs an even intake of calories over the day.

The breakfasts in this chapter will help solve these problems. Microwave Salsa Scramble takes only minutes to prepare and cook. Wake up to a Cocoa Espresso Smoothie and Cheddar Ham Melt. Many can be assembled the night before and finished in the morning in minutes. A steaming bowl of oatmeal flavored with ginger is another microwave breakfast that's packed with flavor. The Blueberry Pancakes, Honey-Walnut French Toast or Banana-Apricot Egg Crepes make perfect weekend breakfasts when you have time to relax and enjoy these tempting dishes.

Choose any of the breakfasts from menus-at-a glance charts on page 20 to 23 and you won't have to think about skipping breakfast. For those of you who can't eat eggs, there are plenty of other choices. Pick and choose any of the breakfasts and you will be having a nutritionally balanced menu.

The average calorie count for the breakfasts in this chapter is 322 with 29 percent of calories from fat.

Apple-Cinnamon Oatmeal • Turkey Cheese Wrap 26

Banana Yogurt–Bran Cup • Roast Beef Open-Faced Sandwich 27

Banana-Apricot Egg Crepes 28

Blueberry Pancakes 29

Breakfast Burrito • Bran Cereal 30

Chorizo Migas (Tex-Mex Eggs with Tortilla Chips) • Bran Cereal 31

Cocoa Espresso Smoothie • Cheddar-Ham Melt 32

Crispy Chinese Pancakes 33

Fresh Herb and Ham Frittata 34

Fruited Cottage Cheese 35

Ginger Oatmeal 36

Good Morning Shake • Melted Cheese Toasts 37

Granola Yogurt Parfait • Cheddar Eggs 38

Ham and Apple Butter Omelet • Banana Bran Cereal 39

Herbed Goat Cheese and Chive Scramble • Blueberry Bran Cereal 40

Honey-Walnut French Toast 41

Hot and Sweet Pepper Rolls 42

Microwave Salsa Scramble • Oatmeal 43

Microwave Spinach and Cheese Scramble • Oatmeal 44

Poached Pesto Eggs • Bran Cereal 45

Smoked Trout Bagel 46

Soft-Cooked Eggs • Bran Cereal 47

Strawberry-Peach Smoothie • Roast Beef Wrap 48

Sun-Dried Tomato and Basil Scramble • Raspberry Bran Cereal 65

Sunnyside-Up Canadian Bacon and Cheese Toast • Bran Cereal 66

Turkey Pastrami on Rye 67

Wild Mushroom Parmesan Omelet • Strawberry Bran Cereal 68

Wild Turkey Hash 69

HELPFUL HINT

- The Turkey Cheese Wrap can be made the night before and refrigerated until needed.

COUNTDOWN

- Make wraps.
- Start oatmeal.
- While oatmeal cooks, prepare the remaining ingredients.

SHOPPING LIST

Dairy

- 1 package sliced, reduced-fat Cheddar cheese

Deli

- Sliced turkey breast (2 ounces needed)

Grocery

- 1 small package pecans (whole or pieces)

Produce

- 1 medium apple

Staples

- Oats
- Ground cinnamon
- Sugar
- Skim milk

APPLE-CINNAMON OATMEAL • TURKEY CHEESE WRAP

Autumn flavors of apples, cinnamon, and pecans are captured in this inviting breakfast, which can be enjoyed any time of the year. Turkey and cheese wraps complete the meal.

Apple-Cinnamon Oatmeal

1 cup oats

1¾ cups water

1 medium apple, cored and sliced (about 1 cup)

½ teaspoon ground cinnamon

2 teaspoons sugar

½ cup skim milk

1 tablespoon pecans pieces

TO PREPARE:

Microwave method: Combine oats and water in a microwaveable bowl. Microwave on high for 3 minutes.

Stove-top method: Combine oats and water in a small saucepan over medium-high heat. Bring to a boil. Reduce heat to medium and cook 5 minutes, stirring occasionally.

To cooked oatmeal, stir in apples, cinnamon, sugar, milk, and pecans. Divide between 2 bowls and serve.

Makes 2 servings

PER SERVING: 247 calories (21 percent from fat), 5.8 g fat (0.8 g saturated, 1.6 g monounsaturated), 1 mg cholesterol, 7.6 g protein, 43.5 g carbohydrates, 6.2 g fiber, 32 mg sodium

Turkey Cheese Wrap

2 ounces sliced turkey breast

2 ounces sliced, reduced-fat Cheddar cheese

Place turkey slices on the countertop. Place slice of cheese on each turkey slice and roll up. If made in advance, wrap in foil or plastic wrap and refrigerate.

Makes 2 servings

PER SERVING: 80 calories (24 percent from fat), 2.2 g fat (1.3 g saturated, 0.6 g monounsaturated), 24 mg cholesterol, 13.9 g protein, 0.5 g carbohydrates, 0 g fiber, 188 mg sodium

BANANA YOGURT–BRAN CUP • ROAST BEEF OPEN-FACED SANDWICH

Banana-flavored yogurt and coconut create a tropical breakfast. A simple roast beef sandwich completes the meal.

Banana Yogurt–Bran Cup

1 cup high-fiber, low-sugar bran cereal

1 cup fat-free, low-sugar, banana-flavored yogurt

2 tablespoons shredded coconut

Divide cereal between 2 bowls. Spoon yogurt over the cereal and sprinkle coconut on top.

Makes 2 servings

PER SERVING: 132 calories (18 percent from fat), 2.6 g fat (1.3 g saturated, 0.1 g monounsaturated), 3 mg cholesterol, 6.2 g protein, 34.7 g carbohydrates, 13.2 g fiber, 205 mg sodium

Roast Beef Open-Faced Sandwich

2 slices whole wheat bread

1 tablespoon reduced-fat mayonnaise

¼ pound sliced, lean deli roast beef

Spread whole wheat bread with mayonnaise. Arrange roast beef on top.

Makes 2 servings

PER SERVING: 203 calories (35 percent from fat), 7.9 g fat (2.2 g saturated, 1.2 g monounsaturated), 49 mg cholesterol, 19.2 g protein, 13.6 g carbohydrates, 1.9 g fiber, 245 mg sodium

This meal contains 335 calories with 28 percent of calories from fat.

HELPFUL HINT

- Strawberry-banana or other banana-flavored yogurt can be used.

COUNTDOWN

- Assemble ingredients.
- Make open-faced roast beef sandwich.
- Make bran cup.

SHOPPING LIST

Dairy

- 1 8-ounce carton fat-free, low-sugar, banana-flavored yogurt

Deli

- Sliced, lean roast beef (¼ pound needed)

Grocery

- 1 small package shredded coconut

Staples

- Whole wheat bread
- Reduced-fat mayonnaise
- High-fiber, low-sugar bran cereal

Photo on page 49.

HELPFUL HINTS

- Look for low-sugar apricot spread with about 10 grams of carbohydrates per tablespoon.

- The size of the skillet is important. It should be 7 to 8 inches in diameter, measured across the flat bottom.

COUNTDOWN

- Assemble ingredients.
- Mix filling.
- Make crepes.

SHOPPING LIST

Dairy

- 1 carton low-fat, low-sodium cottage cheese

Grocery

- 1 jar low-sugar apricot spread
- 1 loaf whole grain bread

Produce

- 1 small banana

Staples

- Eggs
- Sugar
- Olive oil spray

BANANA-APRICOT EGG CREPES

These delicate egg crepes can be made in advance and refrigerated for 1 day, or they can be frozen. Be sure to use a good nonstick skillet for best results.

¾ cup low-fat cottage cheese

2 tablespoons low-sugar apricot spread

½ cup sliced banana

2 large eggs

2 teaspoons sugar

Olive oil spray

2 slices whole grain bread

Mix cottage cheese, apricot spread, and banana together. Set aside.

Break eggs into a small bowl and add sugar. Whisk with a fork. Coat a medium-size nonstick skillet with olive oil spray and place over medium-high heat. Pour half the eggs into the skillet. Rotate the skillet to spread the eggs into a thin layer. Let cook 2 minutes. Turn over for 1 minute. Remove from heat to a plate. Repeat with remaining egg mixture. Divide cottage cheese mixture and place half in the center of each crepe. Fold up lengthwise to make a roll.

Makes 2 servings

PER SERVING: 324 calories (26 percent from fat), 9.5 g fat (3.1 g saturated, 2.9 g monounsaturated), 220 mg cholesterol, 19.9 g protein, 38.7 g carbohydrates, 2.8 g fiber, 553 mg sodium

BLUEBERRY PANCAKES

Pancakes are a weekend favorite. These take only a few minutes to make. They can even be made a day ahead and warmed in the microwave. If they're made ahead, it's best to keep the pancakes and sauce separate until served.

¼ cup water

2 tablespoons sugar

1 cup blueberries, divided use

¼ cup all-purpose flour

⅓ cup reduced-fat ricotta cheese

2 eggs

2 ounces Canadian bacon

Olive oil spray

Place water and sugar in a small saucepan over medium heat. Add ¾ cup blueberries and simmer to dissolve sugar and thicken sauce, about 2 minutes. Set sauce aside.

Mix flour, ricotta cheese, and eggs together. Add the remaining ¼ cup blueberries to the batter. Heat a nonstick skillet over medium heat. Add Canadian bacon and cook 1 to 2 minutes. Remove and divide between 2 plates. Coat the same skillet with olive oil spray. Drop spoonfuls of batter onto hot skillet to form pancakes. Cook 2 minutes. Turn and cook 1 minute. Remove to the plates with the bacon and spoon reserved blueberry sauce on top.

Makes 2 servings

PER SERVING: 341 calories (32 percent from fat), 12.2 g fat (5.0 g saturated, 2.7 g monounsaturated), 248 mg cholesterol, 19.5 g protein, 37.0 g carbohydrates, 2.4 g fiber, 462 mg sodium

This meal contains **341** calories with **32 percent** of calories from fat.

Photo on page 50.

HELPFUL HINT

- This batter makes 6 small 3-inch pancakes or 2 large 6-inch pancakes.

COUNTDOWN

- Assemble ingredients.
- Make blueberry sauce.
- Make pancakes.

SHOPPING LIST

Dairy

- 1 small carton reduced-fat ricotta cheese

Deli

- 1 package Canadian bacon (2 ounces needed)

Produce

- 1 container blueberries

Staples

- Eggs
- All-purpose flour
- Olive oil spray
- Sugar

HELPFUL HINT

- If making ahead, wrap the burrito in plastic wrap or foil and refrigerate. Bring to room temperature before eating.

COUNTDOWN

- Assemble ingredients.
- Make burrito.
- Prepare cereal.

SHOPPING LIST

Dairy

- 1 small carton reduced-fat sour cream

Deli

- 1 package lean deli ham (2 ounces needed)

Grocery

- 1 small container ground cumin
- 1 small can black beans
- 1 small package 6-inch whole wheat tortillas

Produce

- 1 package washed, ready-to-eat spinach

Staples

- Olive oil spray
- Onion
- High-fiber, low-sugar bran cereal
- Skim milk
- Salt
- Black peppercorns

BREAKFAST BURRITO • BRAN CEREAL

Black beans, ham, spinach, and cumin wrapped in tortillas make a tasty, portable breakfast sandwich that can be enjoyed on the run or at home.

Breakfast Burrito

Olive oil spray

½ cup sliced onion

1 cup washed, ready-to-eat spinach

2 ounces lean deli ham

¼ cup canned black beans, rinsed and drained

½ teaspoon ground cumin

Salt and freshly ground black pepper

2 tablespoons reduced-fat sour cream

2 6-inch whole wheat tortillas

Coat a nonstick skillet with olive oil spray and place over medium-high heat. Add onion and cook 2 minutes. Add spinach and ham and stir until spinach is wilted, about 1 minute. Remove from heat and stir in the black beans, cumin, and salt and pepper to taste. Stir in the sour cream.

Warm tortillas in a microwave oven for 10 seconds or place in a toaster oven for 15 to 20 seconds. This will make them easier to roll. Remove tortillas and place on a flat surface. Spread tortillas with black bean mixture. Roll up and place on 2 plates.

Makes 2 servings

PER SERVING: 174 calories (31 percent from fat), 6.0 g fat (2.2 g saturated, 1.4 g monounsaturated), 21 mg cholesterol, 10.6 g protein, 19.9 g carbohydrates, 3.4 g fiber, 441 mg sodium

Bran Cereal

1 cup high-fiber, low-sugar bran cereal

1 cup skim milk

Divide between 2 bowls and serve.

Makes 2 servings

PER SERVING: 103 calories (12 percent from fat), 1.3 g fat (0.2 g saturated, 0.1 g monounsaturated), 3 mg cholesterol, 6.2 g protein, 29.9 g carbohydrates, 13.0 g fiber, 199 mg sodium

CHORIZO MIGAS (TEX-MEX EGGS WITH TORTILLA CHIPS) • BRAN CEREAL

Known in Mexico as Migas (pronounced Mee-gahs), this traditional breakfast dish takes its name from the Spanish word for crumbs—understandable since it always includes scrambled eggs mixed with bits of tortilla or tortilla chips. Chorizo is a spicy Spanish or Mexican pork sausage that lends a very authentic flavor to this dish. Cheese, avocado, and chiles can also be included, if desired.

Tex-Mex Eggs

1 egg

3 egg whites

¼ cup tomato salsa

Salt and freshly ground black pepper

2 tablespoons diced chorizo (½ ounce)

1 cup tortilla chips, broken into ½- to 1-inch pieces

Hot pepper sauce (optional)

Mix whole egg and egg whites in a small bowl. Add salsa and salt and pepper to taste. Set aside. Heat a nonstick skillet over medium heat. Add the chorizo and cook 2 to 3 minutes until it begins to sizzle. Pour the reserved egg mixture into the skillet and scrape with a spatula. When eggs are partially set (about 1 minute), add the tortilla chips and toss gently to combine. Cook to desired doneness. Remove from heat and serve with hot pepper sauce, if desired.

Makes 2 servings

PER SERVING: 175 calories (46 percent from fat), 9.0 g fat (2.5 g saturated, 4.5 g monounsaturated), 113 mg cholesterol, 11.4 g protein, 11.9 g carbohydrates, 1.4 g fiber, 341 mg sodium

Bran Cereal

1 cup high-fiber, low-sugar, bran cereal

1 cup skim milk

Divide between 2 cereal bowls and serve.

Makes 2 servings

PER SERVING: 103 calories (12 percent from fat), 1.3 g fat (0.2 g saturated, 0.1 g monounsaturated), 3 mg cholesterol, 6.2 g protein, 29.9 g carbohydrates, 13.0 g fiber, 199 mg sodium

This meal contains 278 calories with 33 percent of calories from fat.

HELPFUL HINT

- Any type of sausage can be substituted.
- Any type of salsa can be used.

COUNTDOWN

- Assemble ingredients.
- Make cereal.
- Make eggs.

SHOPPING LIST

Deli

- 1 small chorizo sausage

Grocery

- 1 bottle tomato salsa
- 1 small package tortilla chips
- Hot pepper sauce (optional)

Staples

- Eggs
- High-fiber, low-sugar, bran cereal
- Skim milk
- Salt
- Black peppercorns

COCOA ESPRESSO SMOOTHIE • CHEDDAR-HAM MELT

HELPFUL HINTS

- If you like a strong coffee flavor, add another teaspoon instant coffee.
- Egg whites can be used instead of pasteurized liquid egg whites.

COUNTDOWN

- Assemble ingredients.
- Make Cheddar-Ham Melt.

SHOPPING LIST

Dairy

- 1 carton pasteurized liquid egg whites
- 1 small carton half-and-half

Deli

- 1 package lean ham (3 ounces needed)
- 1 package sliced, reduced-fat Cheddar cheese

Grocery

- 1 small bottle instant decaffeinated espresso coffee
- 1 small container unsweetened cocoa powder

Produce

- 1 medium tomato

Staples

- Sugar
- Whole wheat bread

Make this chocolate-flavored coffee smoothie for a quick breakfast drink. Melted Cheddar cheese and ham on toast complete this breakfast.

Cocoa Espresso Smoothie

2 teaspoons instant decaffeinated espresso coffee

2 teaspoons unsweetened cocoa powder

1 tablespoon sugar

½ cup hot water

Pasteurized liquid egg whites equivalent to 2 egg whites

2 tablespoons half-and-half

1 cup ice cubes

Place instant coffee, cocoa powder, sugar, and hot water in a blender. Blend 10 to 15 seconds. Add egg whites, half-and-half, and ice cubes. Blend 30 seconds, or until thick.

Makes 2 servings

PER SERVING: 70 calories (25 percent from fat), 2.0 g fat (1.2 g saturated, 0.6 g monounsaturated), 6 mg cholesterol, 4.5 g protein, 9.0 g carbohydrates, 0.6 g fiber, 15 mg sodium

Cheddar-Ham Melt

2 thin slices reduced-fat Cheddar cheese (2 ounces)

4 slices whole wheat bread

3 ounces lean ham

1 medium tomato, sliced

Place cheese on 2 slices of bread and toast in toaster oven or under broiler until cheese melts. Toast remaining 2 slices at the same time if space permits, or toast separately. Place ham on top of melted cheese and sliced tomatoes on ham. Close with 2 slices toast to make 2 sandwiches.

Makes 2 servings

PER SERVING: 265 calories (23 percent from fat), 6.9 g fat (2.6 g saturated, 2.7 g monounsaturated), 29 mg cholesterol, 22.0 g protein, 30.5 g carbohydrates, 4.9 g fiber, 986 mg sodium

CRISPY CHINESE PANCAKES

Water chestnuts and bean sprouts add a crisp texture to this simple breakfast. It's an especially nice way to break away from the traditional breakfast routine. Be sure to use a good nonstick skillet for best results.

6 ounces peeled, cooked shrimp (1 cup)

2 slices whole wheat bread

2 eggs

2 egg whites

¼ cup sliced water chestnuts

1 cup bean sprouts

2 teaspoons low-sodium soy sauce

Several drops hot-pepper sauce

2 teaspoons sesame oil

Preheat broiler. Cut shrimp into ½-inch chunks. Toast bread. Lightly beat the eggs and egg whites together in a small bowl. Add the water chestnuts, bean sprouts, soy sauce, hot-pepper sauce, and shrimp. Stir. Heat 1 teaspoon sesame oil in an ovenproof, nonstick skillet over medium heat. Add half the mixture and spread out across the skillet, making a thin pancake. When the pancake is firm and a thin golden crust is visible on the edge, about 2 minutes, place skillet under broiler to finish cooking for 1 minute. Remove from broiler, loosen edges with a spatula, and slide onto a plate. Repeat with remaining mixture for second pancake. Serve on plates with toast.

Makes 2 servings

PER SERVING: 331 calories (34 percent from fat), 12.4 g fat (2.7 g saturated, 6.0 g monounsaturated), 342 mg cholesterol, 32.0 g protein, 22.0 g carbohydrates, 2.9 g fiber, 523 mg sodium

This meal contains 331 calories with 34 percent of calories from fat.

HELPFUL HINTS

- Look for canned, sliced water chestnuts.
- Canola oil can be substituted for sesame oil.
- The size of the skillet is important. It should be 7 to 8 inches in diameter, measured across the flat bottom. Make sure it has an ovenproof handle.
- Be careful when removing the skillet from the broiler—the handle will be very hot.

COUNTDOWN

- Preheat broiler.
- Assemble ingredients.
- Make toast.
- Make pancakes.

SHOPPING LIST

Seafood

- 1 package cooked, peeled shrimp (6 ounces needed)

Grocery

- 1 small can sliced water chestnuts
- 1 small bottle sesame oil
- 1 small bottle low-sodium soy sauce

Produce

- 1 small package fresh bean sprouts

Staples

- Eggs
- Hot-pepper sauce
- Whole wheat bread

HELPFUL HINTS

- Use a nonstick skillet with a handle that is oven-proof.
- A quick way to chop chives and parsley is to snip them with a scissors.
- The size of the skillet is important. It should be 7 to 8 inches in diameter, measured across the flat bottom.

COUNTDOWN

- Preheat oven to 400 degrees.
- Start cooking onion, green pepper, and ham.
- Prepare remaining ingredients.
- Make frittata.

SHOPPING LIST

Deli

- 1 package lean ham (4 ounces needed)

Produce

- 1 medium green bell pepper
- 1 bunch fresh chives (or 1 container freeze-dried chives)
- 1 small bunch parsley

Staples

- Onion
- Eggs (6 needed)
- Olive oil
- Whole wheat bread
- Salt
- Black peppercorns

FRESH HERB AND HAM FRITTATA

Cooking frittatas slowly over low heat makes them plump and firm. A frittata needs to be cooked on both sides, so an easy way to do this is to place the frittata in a preheated oven to finish cooking or under a broiler for a minute. They can be made ahead and eaten at room temperature or warmed in a microwave oven.

1 teaspoon olive oil

1 cup sliced onion

1 cup sliced green bell pepper

¼ pound lean ham, torn into bite-size pieces

4 egg whites

2 large whole eggs

¼ cup snipped fresh chives or ½ cup freeze-dried chives

¼ cup snipped parsley

Salt and freshly ground black pepper

2 slices whole wheat bread

Preheat oven to 400 degrees. Heat olive oil in an ovenproof, nonstick skillet over medium-high heat. Add the onion, bell pepper, and ham. Cook 3 minutes. Mix egg whites, whole eggs, chives, and parsley together. Add salt and pepper to taste. Reduce heat to medium and pour egg mixture into skillet. Spread to cover the skillet. Cook to set on the bottom for 3 minutes. Place skillet in the oven for 7 minutes, or until eggs set. If you like drier eggs, leave in oven 1 minute longer. Toast bread and serve with frittata.

Makes 2 servings

PER SERVING: 337 calories (32 percent from fat), 11.8 g fat (3.2 g saturated, 5.6 g monounsaturated), 243 mg cholesterol, 29.5 g protein, 28.7 g carbohydrates, 4.6 g fiber, 909 mg sodium

FRUITED COTTAGE CHEESE

A blend of cinnamon, allspice, and maple syrup add intriguing flavors to this cottage cheese and fruit breakfast. The surprise ingredient here is vinegar. It adds a subtle flavor to the sweet maple syrup.

1½ cups cottage cheese

½ teaspoon ground cinnamon

¼ teaspoon ground allspice

1 apple, cored and sliced (about 1 cup)

1 pear, cored and sliced (about 1 cup)

1½ tablespoons maple syrup

½ tablespoon cider vinegar or water

Spoon cottage cheese into 2 small bowls. Mix cinnamon and allspice into cottage cheese. Place bowl on a dinner plate and arrange apple and pear slices around it. Mix maple syrup and vinegar together and drizzle over fruit.

Makes 2 servings

PER SERVING: 296 calories (25 percent from fat), 8.2 g fat (4.7 g saturated, 2.2 g monounsaturated), 26 mg cholesterol, 21.6 g protein, 35.9 g carbohydrates, 3.9 g fiber, 686 mg sodium

This meal contains 296 calories with 25 percent of calories from fat.

HELPFUL HINT

- Change the fruits with the seasons, using peaches and plums in the summer, for example.

COUNTDOWN

- Assemble ingredients.
- Make dish.

SHOPPING LIST

Dairy

- 1 carton cottage cheese

Grocery

- 1 small bottle cider vinegar
- 1 small bottle maple syrup
- 1 small container ground allspice

Produce

- 1 medium apple
- 1 medium pear

Staples

- Ground cinnamon

HELPFUL HINT

- Crystallized ginger can be found in most supermarkets.

COUNTDOWN

- Assemble ingredients.
- Make oatmeal.

SHOPPING LIST

Grocery

- 1 package crystallized ginger
- 1 carton soy milk
- 1 bottle unsalted, dry-roasted peanuts

Staples

- Oats

GINGER OATMEAL

Ginger, one of the wonders Marco Polo found in Cathay in the 13th century, is still a favorite flavor in many cuisines. Crystallized ginger, which was originally a method of preserving ginger, is now more commonly known as candied ginger. It adds a special flavor to this oatmeal.

1 cup oats

1¾ cups water

1 ounce crystallized ginger, cut into bite-size pieces (scant ¼ cup)

1 cup soy milk

2 tablespoons unsalted, dry-roasted peanuts

TO PREPARE:

Microwave method: Combine oats and water in a microwaveable bowl. Microwave on high for 3 minutes.

Stove-top method: Combine oats and water in a small saucepan over medium-high heat. Bring to a boil. Reduce heat to medium and cook 5 minutes, stirring occasionally.

Mix ginger, soy milk, and peanuts together. Stir into cooked oatmeal.

Makes 2 servings

PER SERVING: 330 calories (29 percent from fat), 10.8 g fat (1.6 g saturated, 3.3 g monounsaturated), 0 mg cholesterol, 13.2 g protein, 48.3 g carbohydrates, 6.5 g fiber, 160 mg sodium

GOOD MORNING SHAKE • MELTED CHEESE TOASTS

This meal contains 331 calories with 29 percent of calories from fat.

Wake up with this orange-flavored milkshake. Melted cheese on toast finishes the meal.

Good Morning Shake

1 cup fat-free, low-sugar orange- or citrus-flavored yogurt

¼ cup orange juice

½ cup skim milk

Pasteurized liquid egg whites equivalent to 2 large eggs

1 cup orange or tangerine segments

Place yogurt, orange juice, skim milk, egg whites, and orange segments in a blender. Blend until smooth.

Makes 2 servings

PER SERVING: 145 calories (2 percent from fat), 0.3 g fat (0.1 g saturated, 0.1 g monounsaturated), 4 mg cholesterol, 10.7 g protein, 25.5 g carbohydrates, 2.2 g fiber, 94 mg sodium

Melted Cheese Toasts

2 ounces sliced, reduced-fat Gruyere cheese

2 slices whole wheat bread

Place cheese on bread and toast in a toaster oven or under the broiler for 1 minute, or until cheese melts and edges of bread are brown.

Makes 2 servings

PER SERVING: 186 calories (50 percent from fat), 10.4 g fat (5.6 g saturated, 3.3 g monounsaturated), 31 mg cholesterol, 11.2 g protein, 13.0 g carbohydrates, 1.9 g fiber, 243 mg sodium

HELPFUL HINTS

- Any type of reduced-fat cheese can be used.
- Canned or bottled orange segments can be used. Make sure they do not have added sugar, and drain them well.
- Egg whites can be used instead of pasteurized egg whites.

COUNTDOWN

- Assemble ingredients.
- Make toast.
- While bread toasts, make shake.

SHOPPING LIST

Dairy

- 1 8-ounce carton pasteurized liquid egg whites
- 1 carton fat-free, low-sugar orange- or citrus-flavored yogurt
- 1 package sliced, reduced-fat Gruyere cheese

Grocery

- 1 small bottle orange juice

Produce

- 2 medium oranges or tangerines

Staples

- Skim milk
- Whole wheat bread

HELPFUL HINTS

- Parfaits are served in tall, narrow glasses, but any type of bowl or glass can be used.

- The parfait can be made the night before and refrigerated until needed.

COUNTDOWN

- Make parfait.
- Make eggs.

SHOPPING LIST

Dairy

- 1 8-ounce carton fat-free, low-sugar vanilla yogurt

- 1 small package sliced, reduced-fat Cheddar cheese

Grocery

- 1 small bottle almond extract

- 1 small package low-fat granola (look for 212 calories per cup)

- 1 small package sliced almonds

Staples

- Eggs
- Olive oil spray
- Salt
- Black peppercorns

GRANOLA YOGURT PARFAIT • CHEDDAR EGGS

In France, parfait means "perfect." Crunchy granola and sliced almonds are layered with yogurt for this simple, perfect breakfast.

Granola Yogurt Parfait

1 cup fat-free, low-sugar vanilla yogurt

¾ teaspoon almond extract

1 cup low-fat granola

2 tablespoons sliced almonds

Mix yogurt and almond extract together. Spoon ¼ cup yogurt mixture into a parfait glass or other small dish. Spoon ½ cup granola over yogurt. Spoon ¼ cup yogurt on top of granola. Sprinkle 1 tablespoon almonds on top. Repeat for second parfait.

Makes 2 servings

PER SERVING: 195 calories (20 percent from fat), 4.3 g fat (0.5 g saturated, 2.5 g monounsaturated), 3 mg cholesterol, 7.5 g protein, 31.9 g carbohydrates, 2.1 g fiber, 161 mg sodium

Cheddar Eggs

2 large eggs

2 ounces sliced, reduced-fat Cheddar cheese, torn into bite-size pieces

Salt and freshly ground black pepper

Olive oil spray

Break eggs into a small bowl. Add cheese and salt and pepper to taste. Whisk with a fork. Heat a nonstick skillet on medium-high heat and coat with olive oil spray. Add egg mixture and scramble. Divide into 2 portions and serve with the parfait.

Makes 2 servings

PER SERVING: 124 calories (51 percent from fat), 7.0 g fat (2.8 g saturated, 2.5 g monounsaturated), 219 mg cholesterol, 13.2 g protein, 1.2 g carbohydrates, 0 g fiber, 237 mg sodium

HAM AND APPLE BUTTER OMELET •
BANANA BRAN CEREAL

Savory ham and apple butter are a nice alternative to cheese and ham in this quick and easy omelet. I prefer to serve my omelets flat because they're faster, but by all means fold your omelets if you prefer. Bran cereal with sliced banana completes the breakfast.

Ham and Apple Butter Omelet

2 whole eggs

4 egg whites

Salt and freshly ground black pepper

Olive oil spray

2 ounces lean deli ham, torn into small pieces (scant ¼ cup)

2 tablespoons apple butter

Beat whole eggs and egg whites together in a small bowl. Add salt and pepper to taste. Heat olive oil in a medium-size nonstick skillet over medium heat. Pour egg mixture into the skillet. Cover with a lid and cook 3 to 4 minutes or until eggs set. Sprinkle ham pieces on half the omelet and spread apple butter over the ham. Remove from heat and hold a plate against the side of the pan. Tilt the pan to allow omelet to slide onto the plate. Cut in half and serve on 2 plates.

Makes 2 servings

PER SERVING: 192 calories (38 percent from fat), 8.1 g fat (2.3 g saturated, 2.7 g monounsaturated), 228 mg cholesterol, 19.2 g protein, 9.0 g carbohydrates, 0.3 g fiber, 415 mg sodium

Banana Bran Cereal

1 cup high-fiber, low-sugar bran cereal

1 cup skim milk

½ cup sliced banana

Divide between 2 bowls and serve.

Makes 2 servings

PER SERVING: 138 calories (10 percent from fat),1.5 g fat (0.2 g saturated, 0.1 g monounsaturated), 3.0 mg cholesterol, 6.6 g protein, 38.7 g carbohydrates, 13.9 g fiber, 199 mg sodium

This meal contains 330 calories with 26 percent of calories from fat.

HELPFUL HINT

- Pasteurized liquid egg whites can be used for the 4 egg whites. Follow the egg equivalent amounts on the carton.

COUNTDOWN

- Assemble ingredients.
- Start omelet.
- While omelet cooks, prepare cereal.
- Finish omelet.

SHOPPING LIST

Deli

- 1 package lean deli ham (2 ounces needed)

Grocery

- 1 jar apple butter

Produce

- 1 small banana

Staples

- Eggs
- Olive oil spray
- High-fiber, low-sugar bran cereal
- Skim milk
- Salt
- Black peppercorns

HELPFUL HINTS

- Any type of goat cheese can be used.
- A quick way to chop chives is to snip them with a scissors.

COUNTDOWN

- Assemble ingredients.
- Prepare the cereal.
- Make the eggs.

SHOPPING LIST

Dairy

- 1 small package herbed goat cheese

Produce

- 1 small bunch chives
- 1 package blueberries

Staples

- Eggs (6 needed)
- Olive oil spray
- High-fiber, low-sugar bran cereal
- Skim milk
- Salt
- Black peppercorns

HERBED GOAT CHEESE AND CHIVE SCRAMBLE • BLUEBERRY BRAN CEREAL

Goat cheese flavored with herbs is a quick way to add a tangy, fresh flavor to scrambled eggs.

Herbed Goat Cheese and Chive Scramble

- 2 whole eggs
- 4 egg whites
- ¼ cup snipped chives
- 1 ounce herbed goat cheese, broken into pieces with a fork
- Salt and freshly ground black pepper
- Olive oil spray

Mix whole eggs, egg whites, chives, and goat cheese together in a small bowl. Stir with a fork to blend in goat cheese. Add salt and pepper to taste. Coat a medium-size nonstick skillet with olive oil spray and place over medium-high heat. Add egg mixture to skillet and scramble 2 minutes, or until they are cooked to desired doneness. Spoon onto 2 plates.

Makes 2 servings

PER SERVING: 175 calories (55 percent from fat), 10.7 g fat (4.7 g saturated, 2.9 g monounsaturated), 224 mg cholesterol, 16.4 g protein, 1.9 g carbohydrates, 0 g fiber, 144 mg sodium

Blueberry Bran Cereal

- 1 cup high-fiber, low-sugar bran cereal
- 1 cup skim milk
- 1 cup blueberries

Divide between 2 bowls and serve.

Makes 2 servings

PER SERVING: 144 calories (10 percent from fat), 1.6 g fat (0.2 g saturated, 0.1 g monounsaturated), 3 mg cholesterol, 6.7 g protein, 40.2 g carbohydrates, 15.0 g fiber, 203 mg sodium

HONEY-WALNUT FRENCH TOAST

Honey, walnuts, and sliced turkey make this a filling breakfast for the weekend or weekday. The secret to good French toast is to make sure the bread soaks up all of the egg.

2 eggs

Salt and freshly ground black pepper

2 slices whole grain bread

Olive oil spray

¼ pound sliced smoked turkey breast

2 tablespoons honey

2 tablespoons walnuts, broken into small pieces

Break eggs into a small bowl. Add salt and pepper to taste. Add the bread and let soak. Turn to make sure both sides soak up the eggs. Coat a large nonstick skillet with olive oil spray and place over medium-high heat. Remove bread from bowl and add to skillet. Cook 2 minutes. Turn and cook another 2 minutes. Remove slices to 2 plates. Divide the turkey between the two slices. Spread honey on turkey and sprinkle walnuts on top.

Makes 2 servings

PER SERVING: 328 calories (35 percent from fat), 12.8 g fat (2.5 g saturated, 3.1 g monounsaturated), 249 mg cholesterol, 24.0 g protein, 31.0 g carbohydrates, 2.2 g fiber, 219 mg sodium

This meal contains 328 calories with 35 percent of calories from fat.

HELPFUL HINT

- Any type of nuts can be used. Break them into small pieces.

COUNTDOWN

- Soak bread in egg.
- Assemble remaining ingredients.
- Make French toast.

SHOPPING LIST

Deli

- 1 package sliced smoked turkey breast (4 ounces needed)

Grocery

- 1 small bottle honey
- 1 small package broken walnuts

Staples

- Whole grain bread
- Eggs
- Olive oil spray
- Salt
- Black peppercorns

HELPFUL HINT

- Any color bell peppers can be used instead of green.

COUNTDOWN

- Preheat broiler or toaster oven.
- Assemble ingredients.
- Make rolls.

SHOPPING LIST

Dairy

- 1 small package shredded mozzarella cheese

Grocery

- 1 small jar sliced roasted red peppers
- 2 whole wheat rolls

Produce

- 1 medium green bell pepper

Staples

- Hot-pepper sauce
- Olive oil spray
- Salt
- Black peppercorns

HOT AND SWEET PEPPER ROLLS

Tantalizingly sweet roasted red pepper, crisp green bell pepper, hot-pepper sauce, and melted cheese make a colorful breakfast sandwich full of tasty contrasts. The heat is up to you on these breakfast rolls. Add the hot-pepper sauce to suit your taste.

½ cup sliced roasted red pepper

½ cup sliced green bell pepper

Several drops hot-pepper sauce

½ cup shredded mozzarella cheese

Salt and freshly ground black pepper

2 whole wheat rolls (about 3 ounces each)

Olive oil spray

Preheat broiler or toaster oven. Mix roasted red pepper and green bell pepper slices together. Add hot-pepper sauce to taste. Toss in mozzarella cheese. Add salt and pepper to taste. Split rolls in half and place on foil-lined baking sheet. Coat with olive oil spray. Spoon filling onto each roll. Place under broiler for 2 minutes or until cheese melts. Serve as open-faced sandwich.

Makes 2 servings

PER SERVING: 336 calories (30 percent from fat), 11.2 g fat (4.8 g saturated, 3.1 g monounsaturated), 21 mg cholesterol, 18 g protein, 44.6 g carbohydrates, 7.1 g fiber, 623 mg sodium

MICROWAVE SALSA SCRAMBLE • OATMEAL

Make these delightfully fluffy scrambled eggs in 3 minutes, with no skillet to wash. You can even make these ahead of time and refrigerate overnight. Warm them in a microwave for about 30 seconds or eat them at room temperature.

Microwave Salsa Scramble

2 whole eggs

4 egg whites

½ cup no-sugar-added tomato salsa

Salt and freshly ground black pepper

With a fork, stir 1 whole egg and 2 egg whites in a microwaveable bowl or ramekin. Cover with a paper towel and microwave on high 1 minute. Remove from the microwave oven and stir. Microwave for 30 seconds. Remove and stir in ¼ cup salsa. Add salt and pepper to taste. Repeat with a second bowl and remaining ingredients.

Makes 2 servings

PER SERVING: 127 calories (37 percent from fat), 5.2 g fat (1.6 g saturated, 1.9 g monounsaturated), 213 mg cholesterol, 14.0 g protein, 5.3 g carbohydrates, 1.0 g fiber, 352 mg sodium

Oatmeal

1 cup oats

1 cup skim milk

TO PREPARE:

Microwave method: Combine oats and milk in a microwaveable bowl. Microwave on high for 3 minutes.

Stove-top method: Combine oats and milk in a small saucepan over medium-high heat. Bring to a boil. Reduce heat to medium and cook 5 minutes, stirring occasionally.

Makes 2 servings

PER SERVING: 193 calories (19 percent from fat), 3.0 g fat (0.7 g saturated, 0.1 g monounsaturated), 3 mg cholesterol, 9.2 g protein, 32 g carbohydrates, 4.0 g fiber, 64 mg sodium

This meal contains 320 calories with 23 percent of calories from fat.

HELPFUL HINT

- Timing can vary for microwave ovens. Test the timing given here, then alter if necessary.

COUNTDOWN

- Assemble ingredients.
- Make oatmeal.
- Make eggs.

SHOPPING LIST

Grocery

- 1 small jar no-sugar-added tomato salsa

Staples

- Eggs
- Oats
- Skim milk
- Salt
- Black peppercorns

HELPFUL HINT

- Timing can vary for microwave ovens. Test the timing given here, then alter accordingly.

COUNTDOWN

- Assemble ingredients.
- Prepare oatmeal.
- Make eggs.

SHOPPING LIST

Dairy

- 1 small package reduced-fat, shredded, sharp Cheddar cheese

Produce

- 1 package washed, ready-to-eat baby spinach

Staples

- Eggs (6 needed)
- Oats
- Skim milk
- Salt
- Black peppercorns

MICROWAVE SPINACH AND CHEESE SCRAMBLE • OATMEAL

Fresh spinach and shredded, sharp Cheddar cheese add intense flavor and color to these 3-minute microwaved eggs.

Microwave Spinach and Cheese Scramble

2 whole eggs

4 egg whites

1 cup washed, ready-to-eat baby spinach

Salt and freshly ground black pepper

2 ounces reduced-fat, shredded, sharp Cheddar cheese (about ¾ cup)

With a fork, stir 1 whole egg and 2 egg whites in a microwaveable bowl or ramekin. Add ½ cup spinach and salt and pepper to taste. Cover with a paper towel and microwave on high 1 minute. Remove from the microwave oven, stir, and sprinkle half of the shredded cheese on top. Microwave for 30 seconds. Stir and serve. Repeat with a second bowl and remaining ingredients.

Makes 2 servings

PER SERVING: 162 calories (39 percent from fat), 7.1 g fat (2.8 g saturated, 2.5 g monounsaturated), 219 mg cholesterol, 20.5 g protein, 2.4 g carbohydrates, 0.4 g fiber, 257 mg sodium

Oatmeal

1 cup oats

1 cup skim milk

TO PREPARE:

Microwave method: Combine oats and milk in a microwaveable bowl. Microwave on high for 3 minutes.

Stove-top method: Combine oats and milk in a small saucepan over medium-high heat. Bring to a boil. Reduce heat to medium and cook 5 minutes, stirring occasionally.

Makes 2 servings

PER SERVING: 193 calories (19 percent from fat), 3.0 g fat (0.7 g saturated, 0.1 g monounsaturated), 3 mg cholesterol, 9.2 g protein, 32 g carbohydrates, 4.0 g fiber, 64 mg sodium

POACHED PESTO EGGS • BRAN CEREAL

To poach is to cook gently in liquid, and the goal whenever an egg is concerned is to produce a just-set white with a neat round shape. Sometimes the shape is helped by trimming away trailing bits of cooked white. A little lemon juice or vinegar added to the poaching liquid helps to coagulate the white and preserve the shape of the egg. It will, however, flavor the egg. Add 1 to 2 teaspoons if you prefer a rounded egg.

The real beauty of this style egg is that it can be made a day ahead, if necessary, and rewarmed. See Helpful Hints for directions on how to do this.

Poached Pesto Eggs

- 2 slices rye bread
- 1 tablespoon prepared pesto sauce
- 2 large eggs

Bring a large saucepan three-quarters full of water to a boil over high heat. Meanwhile, toast bread and spread each slice with pesto sauce. Place on 2 plates.

When water boils, reduce heat to medium-low so water just simmers. Break an egg into a small cup without breaking the yolk. Slide into bubbling water. Repeat with second egg. Reduce heat to low and poach eggs, uncovered, for 3 minutes. Gently lift eggs out of water with a slotted spoon, drain well, and place each egg on pesto toast.

Makes 2 servings

PER SERVING: 196 calories (43 percent from fat), 9.3 g fat (2.5 g saturated, 4.7 g monounsaturated), 216 mg cholesterol, 9.9 g protein, 17 g carbohydrates, 2.2 g fiber, 347 mg sodium

Bran Cereal

- 1 cup high-fiber, low-sugar bran cereal
- 1 cup skim milk

Divide between 2 bowls and serve.

Makes 2 servings

PER SERVING: 103 calories (12 percent from fat), 1.3 g fat (0.2 g saturated, 0.1 g monounsaturated), 3 mg cholesterol, 6.2 g protein, 29.9 g carbohydrates, 13.0 g fiber, 199 mg sodium

This meal contains 299 calories with 32 percent of calories from fat.

HELPFUL HINTS

- Lift each egg carefully from the pan with slotted spoon. The white should be firm and the yolk soft.

- To make ahead, transfer the poached eggs to a bowl of ice water and store in the refrigerator. To reheat, transfer eggs to bowl of water just hot to touch and let stand 5 to 10 minutes. Drain on paper towel.

COUNTDOWN

- Place water for eggs on to boil.
- Toast bread.
- Poach eggs.
- Assemble dish.

SHOPPING LIST

Grocery

- 1 container prepared pesto sauce

Staples

- Eggs
- Rye bread
- High-fiber, low-sugar bran cereal
- Skim milk

This meal contains 326
calories with 25 percent
of calories from fat.

HELPFUL HINTS

- Buy bagels that are
  about 3 inches in
  diameter or the size of a
  coffee jar lid.

- Any type of smoked fish
  can be used, except
  smoked salmon if you're
  watching calories closely.

COUNTDOWN

- Assemble ingredients.
- Make bagel sandwich.

SHOPPING LIST

Dairy

- 1 small package cream
  cheese

Seafood

- 1 package smoked trout
  fillet (¼ pound needed)

Grocery

- 2 small oat bran or whole
  wheat bagels

- 1 bottle prepared
  horseradish

SMOKED TROUT BAGEL

Bagels and cream cheese are one of America's favorite breakfasts. Here's a version that won't break the calorie bank.

2 oat bran or whole
   wheat bagels, about 3
   inches in diameter,
   sliced (3 ounces each)

2 tablespoons cream
   cheese (about 1 ounce)

1 tablespoon prepared
   horseradish

¼ pound smoked trout
   fillet

Remove some of the soft bread from the inside of the bagel. Toast bagels. Mix cream cheese and horseradish together. Spread on bottom half of both bagels. Divide the smoked trout between the 2 bagels. Close with the top half.

Makes 2 servings

PER SERVING: 326 calories (25 percent from fat), 9.1 g fat (4.0 g saturated, 2.9 g monounsaturated), 60 mg cholesterol, 23.6 g protein, 40.0 g carbohydrates, 6.0 g fiber, 942 mg sodium

SOFT-COOKED EGGS • BRAN CEREAL

A simple, soft-cooked egg, perfectly cooked, makes a delicious and quick breakfast that is an especially nice alternative to hard-boiled eggs. The secret to soft-cooked eggs is to make sure the water is kept at a very low simmer. Boiling the water will make the eggs rubbery.

Soft-Cooked Eggs

2 slices whole wheat bread

4 eggs, at room temperature

Toast bread and place on 2 plates. Fill a pan with enough water to cover eggs by 1 inch. Bring water to a gentle simmer over medium heat. (The bubbles should just barely break the surface.) Lower the eggs with slotted spoon into the water. Simmer 3 minutes for very runny eggs and 5 minutes for firmer eggs. Serve egg in the shell in an egg cup, cracking the top lightly with spoon and peeling away about ½ inch of shell. Or cut the egg in half and use a spoon to scoop the egg into a small, warm dish or over the toast. Serve with the toast.

Makes 2 servings

PER SERVING: 219 calories (46 percent from fat), 11.2 g fat (3.4 g saturated, 4.3 g monounsaturated), 426 mg cholesterol, 15.2 g protein, 14.1 g carbohydrates, 1.9 g fiber, 274 mg sodium

Bran Cereal

1 cup high-fiber, low-sugar bran cereal

1 cup skim milk

Divide between 2 bowls and serve.

Makes 2 servings

PER SERVING: 103 calories (12 percent from fat), 1.3 g fat (0.2 g saturated, 0.1 g monounsaturated), 3 mg cholesterol, 6.2 g protein, 29.9 g carbohydrates, 13.0 g fiber, 199 mg sodium

This meal contains 322 calories with 35 percent of calories from fat.

HELPFUL HINT

- The eggs should be at room temperature before placing them in the simmering water, to avoid cracking. If they are cold, place them in a bowl of warm water for a minute.

COUNTDOWN

- Assemble ingredients.
- Toast bread.
- Cook eggs.
- While eggs cook, prepare cereal.

SHOPPING LIST

Staples

- Eggs
- Whole wheat bread
- High-fiber, low-sugar bran cereal
- Skim milk

Photo on page 51.

HELPFUL HINT

- If using frozen strawberries or peaches, make sure they are not packed in a sugar syrup.

COUNTDOWN

- Assemble ingredients.
- Make wrap.
- Make smoothie.

SHOPPING LIST

Dairy

- 1 8-ounce carton fat-free, low-sugar strawberry yogurt
- 1 container pasteurized liquid egg whites

Deli

- Sliced, lean deli roast beef (¼ pound needed)

Grocery

- 1 package 8-inch whole wheat tortillas

Produce

- 1 container fresh strawberries or 1 package frozen strawberries
- 1 medium ripe peach or 1 package frozen peach slices
- 1 medium tomato

Staples

- Vanilla extract
- Sugar
- Dijon mustard

STRAWBERRY-PEACH SMOOTHIE • ROAST BEEF WRAP

Assemble this thick and creamy drink in minutes—or do it the night before. In the morning, add the ice, blend it, and take it on the run. Many smoothies are high in calories and low on protein. This one is balanced and packed with flavor.

Strawberry-Peach Smoothie

1 cup fresh or frozen strawberries

1 medium ripe peach, pitted and quartered, or 1 cup frozen peach slices

1 cup fat-free, low-sugar strawberry yogurt

Pasteurized liquid egg whites equivalent to 2 egg whites

2 teaspoons vanilla extract

1 tablespoon sugar

1 cup ice cubes

Place strawberries, peach slices, yogurt, egg whites, vanilla extract, and sugar in a blender. Blend until smooth. Add the ice cubes and blend until thick. Pour into 2 glasses.

Makes 2 servings

PER SERVING: 159 calories (3 percent from fat), 0.5 g fat (0 g saturated, 0.1 g monounsaturated), 3 mg cholesterol, 8.7 g protein, 29.1 g carbohydrates, 3.0 g fiber, 63 mg sodium

Roast Beef Wrap

1 tablespoon Dijon mustard

1 8-inch whole wheat tortilla

¼ pound sliced, lean deli roast beef

1 tomato, sliced

Spread mustard over tortilla. Place roast beef over mustard and top with sliced tomatoes. Roll up and cut in half. Serve one half with each smoothie.

Makes 2 servings

PER SERVING: 172 calories (28 percent from fat), 5.5 g fat (1.9 g saturated, 0.2 g monounsaturated), 46 mg cholesterol, 18.8 g protein, 11.6 g carbohydrates, 2.3 g fiber, 196 mg sodium

BANANA-APRICOT EGG CREPES • page 28

BLUEBERRY PANCAKES • page 29

STRAWBERRY-PEACH SMOOTHIE AND ROAST BEEF WRAP • page 48

ASIAN-MEXICAN TOSTADOS • page 72

BLACK BEAN, COUSCOUS, AND PEPPER SALAD • page 76

SHRIMP AND PEACH PASTA SALAD • page 112

TEXAS TUNA BURGER WITH JALAPEÑO MAYONNAISE • page 118

CRAB SCAMPI AND SPAGHETTI • page 134

HALIBUT IN CIDER AND SAFFRON RICE • page 138

CURRY-KISSED CHICKEN AND CARROTS AND RICE • page 156

CHINESE PORK IN LETTUCE PUFFS • page 174

MEXICAN PORK AND BEAN CHILI • page 176

WALNUT-CRUSTED STEAK AND FENNEL BEAN SALAD • page 188

PLUM MERINGUE • page 198

BARBECUED KOREAN CHICKEN, SWEET POTATO SALAD, AND BROCCOLI SLAW (*front*)
with SORBET CUP (*back*) • pages 213, 214, and 215

MIXED FRUIT TART • page 222

SUN-DRIED TOMATO AND BASIL SCRAMBLE • RASPBERRY BRAN CEREAL

Sun-dried tomatoes and basil give these eggs the flavor of sunny Tuscany. Use sun-dried tomatoes packed in olive oil and drain well. Fresh raspberries provide the perfect contrast to the intense, bright flavors of the tomatoes.

Sun-Dried Tomato and Basil Scramble

2 whole eggs

4 egg whites

Olive oil spray

⅓ cup chopped sun-dried tomatoes in olive oil, drained

⅓ cup fresh basil leaves, torn into small pieces

Salt and freshly ground black pepper

Break whole eggs and egg whites in a medium-size bowl. Add salt and pepper to taste and beat with a fork. Coat a medium-size nonstick skillet with olive oil spray and place over medium-high heat. Add egg mixture to skillet and scramble 1 minute. Add the sun-dried tomatoes and basil and continue to scramble about 1 minute longer, until eggs are cooked. Spoon onto 2 plates.

Makes 2 servings

PER SERVING: 163 calories (50 percent from fat), 9.1 g fat (2.1 g saturated, 3.5 g monounsaturated), 213 mg cholesterol, 14.3 g protein, 5.8 g carbohydrates, 1.3 g fiber, 120 mg sodium

Raspberry Bran Cereal

1 cup high-fiber, low-sugar bran cereal

1 cup skim milk

1 cup raspberries

Divide between 2 bowls and serve.

Makes 2 servings

PER SERVING: 134 calories (11 percent from fat), 1.7 g fat (0.2 g saturated, 0.1 g monounsaturated), 3 mg cholesterol, 6.7 g protein, 37.0 g carbohydrates, 15.9 g fiber, 199 mg sodium

This meal contains 297 calories with 33 percent of calories from fat.

HELPFUL HINT

- Buy sliced or chopped sun-dried tomatoes, drain well, and pat dry with a paper towel.

COUNTDOWN

- Assemble ingredients.
- Make eggs.
- Prepare cereal.

SHOPPING LIST

Grocery

- 1 small jar sliced sun-dried tomatoes packed in olive oil

Produce

- 1 container raspberries
- 1 small bunch fresh basil leaves

Staples

- Eggs
- Olive oil spray
- Salt
- Black peppercorns
- High-fiber, low-sugar bran cereal
- Skim milk

SUNNYSIDE-UP CANADIAN BACON AND CHEESE TOAST • BRAN CEREAL

This is an open-faced sandwich with the eggs cooked on a slice of Canadian bacon and served on toast. For those who love eggs Benedict, this dish delivers some similar flavors—with far less fat because the Hollandaise is omitted.

Sunnyside-Up Canadian Bacon and Cheese Toast

2 slices Canadian bacon (2 ounces)

2 large eggs
  Salt and freshly ground black pepper

2 thin slices reduced-fat sharp Cheddar cheese (2 ounces)

2 slices whole wheat bread

Heat a nonstick skillet over medium-high heat. Add the Canadian bacon. Cook 1 minute and turn. Break 1 egg onto each slice. Sprinkle the egg with salt and pepper to taste. Place 1 slice of cheese over each egg. Cover skillet with a lid and cook 4 to 5 minutes, or until the egg whites are just set. While eggs cook, toast the bread. Place the toast on 2 plates and gently place the bacon and egg on the toast.

Makes 2 servings

PER SERVING: 234 calories (37 percent from fat), 9.7 g fat (3.6 g saturated, 3.7 g monounsaturated), 234 mg cholesterol, 21.8 g protein, 14.5 g carbohydrates, 1.9 g fiber, 726 mg sodium

Bran Cereal

1 cup high fiber, low-sugar bran cereal

1 cup skim milk

Divide between 2 bowls and serve.

Makes 2 servings

PER SERVING: 103 calories (12 percent from fat), 1.3 g fat (0.2 g saturated, 0.1 g monounsaturated), 3 mg cholesterol, 6.2 g protein, 29.9 g carbohydrates, 13.0 g fiber, 199 mg sodium

TURKEY PASTRAMI ON RYE

Many people tell me they're allergic to or can't have eggs. This breakfast-style sandwich is perfect for them. Especially great for taking on the run, it can be assembled the night before so it's ready for a quick pass beneath the broiler before you dash out the door.

4 slices rye bread

2 tablespoons Dijon mustard

¼ pound sliced turkey pastrami

¼ cup shredded Swiss cheese (about 1 ounce)

1 small tomato, sliced

Preheat broiler or toaster oven. Line a baking sheet with foil. Place bread on the sheet. Spread mustard on the bread. Place turkey pastrami on 2 slices. Place Swiss cheese over turkey pastrami. Place under broiler for 1 minute, or until cheese melts. Place tomato slices over cheese and close sandwich with other 2 slices bread.

Makes 2 servings

PER SERVING: 305 calories (20 percent from fat), 6.8 g fat (3.0 g saturated, 2.3 g monounsaturated), 48 mg cholesterol, 24.6 g protein, 35.7 g carbohydrates, 5.4 g fiber, 658 mg sodium

This meal contains 305 calories with 20 percent of calories from fat.

HELPFUL HINT

- Smoked turkey breast can be substituted for turkey pastrami if you prefer.

COUNTDOWN

- Preheat broiler.
- Assemble ingredients.
- Make sandwich.

SHOPPING LIST

Deli

- Sliced turkey pastrami (¼ pound needed)
- 1 package shredded Swiss cheese

Produce

- 1 small tomato

Staples

- Dijon mustard
- Rye bread

HELPFUL HINTS

- Buy good-quality Parmesan cheese and chop or grate it in the food processor. Freeze extra for quick use. You can quickly spoon out what you need and leave the rest frozen.

- The best way to clean mushrooms is to wipe them with a damp paper towel. They can absorb too much water if washed under running water.

COUNTDOWN

- Assemble ingredients.
- Make omelet.
- Prepare cereal.

SHOPPING LIST

Dairy

- 1 small package Parmesan cheese

Produce

- 1 small package sliced portobello mushrooms
- 1 small package shiitake mushrooms
- 1 small package strawberries

Staples

- Eggs (6 needed)
- Olive oil spray
- Onion
- High-fiber, low-sugar bran cereal
- Skim milk
- Salt
- Black peppercorns

WILD MUSHROOM PARMESAN OMELET • STRAWBERRY BRAN CEREAL

An omelet with a golden top and creamy center is a treat. It's easy to make and takes only minutes.

Wild Mushroom Parmesan Omelet

- 2 whole eggs
- 4 egg whites
- 2 tablespoons grated Parmesan cheese
  Salt and freshly ground black pepper
  Olive oil spray
- 2 ounces portobello mushrooms, sliced (1 scant cup)
- 2 ounces shiitake mushrooms, sliced (1 scant cup)
- 1 cup sliced onion

Beat whole eggs, egg whites, and Parmesan cheese together in a medium-size bowl. Add salt and pepper to taste. Heat a medium-size nonstick skillet over medium-high heat and coat with olive oil spray. Add the mushrooms and onion. Cook 3 to 4 minutes. Sprinkle with salt and pepper to taste. Remove mushroom mixture to a plate. Pour egg mixture into the skillet. Cover with a lid and cook 3 to 4 minutes, or until eggs set. Spread the mushrooms on half the omelet and fold the omelet in half. Slide out of the pan by tipping the pan and holding a plate against the side of the pan. Cut in half and serve on 2 plates.

Makes 2 servings

PER SERVING: 194 calories (37 percent from fat), 8.3 g fat (2.8 g saturated, 2.4 g monounsaturated), 217 mg cholesterol, 17.7 g protein, 12.0 g carbohydrates, 1.8 g fiber, 169 mg sodium

Strawberry Bran Cereal

- 1 cup high-fiber, low-sugar bran cereal
- 1 cup strawberries, hulled and washed
- 1 cup skim milk

Divide between 2 cereal bowls and serve.

Makes 2 servings

PER SERVING: 126 calories (12 percent from fat), 1.6 g fat (0.2 g saturated, 0.1 g monounsaturated), 3 mg cholesterol, 6.6 g protein, 35.3 g carbohydrates, 14.8 g fiber, 200 mg sodium

WILD TURKEY HASH

This meal contains 324 calories with 30 percent of calories from fat.

Hash is a great American comfort food. Here is a quick and easy version with turkey, mushrooms, onion, potato, and bell peppers. While the vegetables sizzle on the stove, the potatoes get a head start cooking in the microwave. A luscious spoonful of heavy cream helps bind ingredients together.

¼ whole grain French baguette

¼ pound red potatoes, unpeeled (about ¾ cup cubed)

3 teaspoons olive oil

½ cup sliced red onion

½ cup sliced red bell pepper

½ cup sliced shiitake mushrooms

¼ pound smoked deli turkey breast, cut into cubes

1 tablespoon all-purpose flour

¼ cup skim milk

1 tablespoon heavy cream

Salt and freshly ground black pepper

Preheat oven or toaster oven to 300 degrees. Place bread in oven to warm. Wash potatoes and cut into ½-inch cubes. Place in microwaveable bowl, cover with paper towel, and microwave on high 2 minutes. Meanwhile, heat oil in a nonstick skillet over medium-high heat. Add potatoes, onion, red bell pepper, and mushrooms. Cook 3 minutes. Add turkey and cook 2 minutes longer. Push ingredients to the sides of the skillet, leaving a hole in the center. Add flour and then milk. Stir to mix. Toss with the ingredients. The sauce will lightly bind the hash together. Add cream and toss again. Add salt and pepper to taste. Remove bread from oven, slice, and serve with hash.

Makes 2 servings

PER SERVING: 324 calories (30 percent from fat), 10.9 g fat (3.0 g saturated, 6.2 g monounsaturated), 47 mg cholesterol, 20.5 g protein, 36.6 g carbohydrates, 3.4 g fiber, 187 mg sodium

HELPFUL HINT

- Ask the deli to cut the turkey into 1 thick slice. This makes it easier to cut into cubes.

COUNTDOWN

- Preheat oven or toaster oven to 300 degrees.
- Start potatoes.
- Assemble remaining ingredients.
- Make hash.

SHOPPING LIST

Dairy

- 1 small carton heavy cream

Deli

- Smoked deli turkey breast (¼ pound needed)

Grocery

- 1 small whole grain French baguette

Produce

- ¼ pound red potatoes
- 1 medium red bell pepper
- 1 small package shiitake mushrooms

Staples

- Olive oil
- Red onion
- All-purpose flour
- Skim milk
- Salt
- Black peppercorns

LUNCH

Whether it's lunch on the run, at your desk, or with friends, you'll find a wide variety of lunches here to fit your lifestyle. The menus-at-a-glance starting on page 20 list the quicker lunches for weekdays and the more special ones for the weekends. All of the lunches are fast and easy. The ingredients can be bought during a brief stop at your local supermarket. The lunches in this chapter average 444 calories with 26 percent of calories from fat. Meals emphasize fruits, vegetables, whole grains, and lean protein, and are low in saturated fats, trans fats, cholesterol, sodium, and added sugars.

Photo on page 52.

HELPFUL HINTS

- White vinegar diluted with a little water can be used instead of rice vinegar.

- Any type of sliced mushrooms can be used instead of shiitake mushrooms.

- There are many types of Thai peanut sauce. I prefer a thicker one for this recipe.

COUNTDOWN

- Preheat broiler.
- Prepare ingredients.
- Complete dish.

ASIAN-MEXICAN TOSTADOS

Tostados are a traditional Mexican dish made with crisply fried corn tortillas topped with a variety of fillings. In this new twist, hot Thai peanut sauce and shiitake mushrooms top broiled tortillas. Roasted chicken strips and lettuce provide a lovely contrast to the simple, tangy filling.

Olive oil spray

4 6-inch corn tortillas

1 teaspoon Chinese vinegar

1 teaspoon sesame oil

½ cup shredded lettuce

3 shiitake mushrooms, sliced (about ½ cup)

½ pound cooked, boneless, skinless chicken breasts, cut into strips

4 tablespoons Thai peanut sauce

1 small tomato, chopped (about 1 cup)

Preheat broiler. Line a baking sheet with foil and coat with olive oil spray. Spray both sides of tortillas and place on sheet. Broil 1 minute. Turn tortillas over and broil 30 seconds or until crisp, but not brown. Remove from broiler.

Mix Chinese vinegar and sesame oil in a small bowl. Add lettuce and shiitake mushrooms and toss well. Divide evenly over 4 tortillas. Using the same bowl, toss chicken in peanut sauce and spoon over vegetables on the tortillas. Sprinkle tomatoes on top.

Makes 2 servings

PER SERVING: 346 calories (29 percent from fat), 11.3 g fat (2.1 g saturated, 2.1 g monounsaturated), 73 mg cholesterol, 34.8 g protein, 20.7 g carbohydrates, 4.0 g fiber, 611 mg sodium

Dessert

2 small bananas

Makes 2 servings

PER SERVING: 117 calories (5 percent from fat), 0.6 g fat (0.2 g saturated, 0.1 g monounsaturated), 0 mg cholesterol, 1.3 g protein, 29.9 g carbohydrates, 3.1 g fiber, 2 mg sodium

Meat

- 1 package cooked, boneless, skinless chicken breasts cut into strips (8 ounces needed)

Grocery

- 1 package 6-inch corn tortillas
- 1 small bottle Chinese vinegar
- 1 small bottle sesame oil
- 1 small bottle Thai peanut sauce

Produce

- 1 small package shredded lettuce
- 1 small package shiitake mushrooms
- 1 small tomato
- 2 small bananas

Staples

- Olive oil spray

BARBECUED CHICKEN SANDWICH

This juicy sandwich is made with chicken tenderloins, the finest part of the chicken breast. Tenderloins cook quickly due to their small size. They can be found packaged in most supermarkets.

4 slices multigrain bread

2 teaspoons canola oil

½ pound boneless, skinless chicken tenderloins

½ cup low-sugar barbecue sauce

2 medium tomatoes, sliced

¼ cup diced red onion

1 tablespoon reduced-fat oil and vinegar dressing

Toast bread and place 1 slice each on 2 plates. Heat oil in a nonstick skillet over medium-high heat. Add chicken and cook 3 minutes. Lower heat to medium and turn chicken over. Spoon barbecue sauce over the cooked side. Continue to cook 2 minutes. Spoon chicken and sauce on the slices of bread on the plates. Cover each with the remaining bread and cut the sandwiches in half. Place tomato slices on the 2 plates and sprinkle with onion. Drizzle dressing over tomatoes.

Makes 2 servings

PER SERVING: 434 calories (21 percent from fat), 10.0 g fat (1.7 g saturated, 4.7 g monounsaturated), 64 mg cholesterol, 33.8 g protein, 53.3 g carbohydrates, 7.0 g fiber, 1,323 mg sodium

Dessert

2   medium apples

Makes 2 servings

PER SERVING: 81 calories (6 percent from fat), 0.5 g fat (0.1 g saturated, 0 g monounsaturated), 0 mg cholesterol, 0.3 g protein, 20.9 g carbohydrates, 3.7 g fiber, 0 mg sodium

SHOPPING LIST

Meat

- 1 package boneless, skinless chicken tenderloins (8 ounces needed)

Grocery

- 1 small bottle low-sugar barbecue sauce (look for one that has about 11 grams carbohydrates for 2 tablespoons)

Produce

- 2 medium tomatoes
- 2 medium apples

Staples

- Multigrain bread
- Canola oil
- Red onion
- Reduced-fat oil and vinegar dressing

This meal contains 519 calories with 29 percent of calories from fat.

Photo on page 53.

HELPFUL HINTS

- At the deli counter, ask for the ham to be cut in one thick piece so that it can be easily cut into ½-inch cubes or coarsely chopped.
- Parsley can be substituted for the cilantro.

COUNTDOWN

- Make couscous.
- Prepare ingredients.
- Assemble salad.

BLACK BEAN, COUSCOUS, AND PEPPER SALAD

This is a simple salad using quick-cooking couscous. It can be made the night before and refrigerated until needed. The flavor will improve with age.

¾ cup water

2 teaspoons olive oil

½ cup quick-cooking couscous

½ cup rinsed and drained canned black beans

¼ pound lean ham, coarsely chopped

½ cup diced red onion

1 medium red bell pepper, coarsely chopped (about 1 cup)

2 tablespoons olive oil and vinegar dressing

Several drops hot-pepper sauce

Salt and freshly ground black pepper

½ cup chopped fresh cilantro

Several lettuce leaves (optional)

Bring water and olive oil to a boil. Remove from the heat, add couscous, stir, and cover with a lid. Let stand 5 minutes.

Place black beans, ham, onion, and red bell pepper in a medium-size bowl. Add the couscous. Drizzle dressing over salad. Add hot-pepper sauce and salt and pepper to taste. Toss well. Sprinkle cilantro on top. To serve, arrange lettuce leaves on 2 plates and spoon salad onto the lettuce.

Makes 2 servings

PER SERVING: 444 calories (33 percent from fat), 16.3 g fat (3.2 g saturated, 7.2 g monounsaturated), 30 mg cholesterol, 22.2 g protein, 52.8 g carbohydrates, 7.0 g fiber, 698 mg sodium

Dessert

4 medium tangerines

Makes 2 servings

PER SERVING: 74.8 calories (4 percent from fat), 0.3 g fat (0 g saturated, 0.1 g monounsaturated), 0 mg cholesterol, 1.1 g protein, 19.0 g carbohydrates, 3.9 g fiber, 2 mg sodium

SHOPPING LIST

Deli

- Lean ham, preferably one piece (¼ pound needed)

Grocery

- 1 small package quick-cooking couscous
- 1 can black beans

Produce

- 1 medium red bell pepper
- 1 small bunch cilantro
- 1 small head lettuce (optional)
- 4 medium tangerines

Staples

- Olive oil
- Red onion
- Olive oil and vinegar dressing
- Hot-pepper sauce
- Salt
- Black peppercorns

HELPFUL HINTS

- Any type of lettuce can be used.

- When layering the ingredients, leave about 2 inches from the top of the tortilla. As you roll the tortilla, the ingredients will slide forward.

COUNTDOWN

- Assemble the grapes.

- Make wrap.

CLUB SANDWICH WRAP

This sandwich can be made a day ahead, wrapped in foil, and refrigerated. However, if you choose that option, you may also want to reorder the ingredients so the cheese is placed on the tortilla first; then your wrap will not become soggy. Bring it to room temperature before serving.

2 tablespoons Dijon mustard

1 tablespoon reduced-fat mayonnaise

2 10-inch whole wheat tortillas

1 medium tomato, sliced

¼ pound sliced, low-salt deli turkey

2 ounces reduced-fat Swiss cheese

2 slices Canadian bacon (about 2 ounces)

1 cup washed, ready-to-eat shredded lettuce

Mix mustard and mayonnaise together. Spread over the tortillas. Place tomato slices over the mayonnaise and mustard. Place a slice of turkey, a slice of cheese, and a slice of Canadian bacon on each tortilla. Place shredded lettuce over the bacon. Fold in the ends and roll up lengthwise to make the wrap.

Makes 2 servings

PER SERVING: 366 calories (28 percent from fat), 11.2 g fat (4.3 g saturated, 1.9 g monounsaturated), 69 mg cholesterol, 35.5 g protein, 29.4 g carbohydrates, 5.1 g fiber, 864 mg sodium

Dessert

2 cups seedless red grapes

Divide between 2 dessert bowls.

Makes 2 servings

PER SERVING: 62 calories (4 percent from fat), 0.3 g fat (0.1 g saturated, 0 g monounsaturated), 0 mg cholesterol, 0.6 g protein, 15.8 g carbohydrates, 0.9 g fiber, 2 mg sodium

SHOPPING LIST

Deli

- Sliced, low-salt deli turkey (¼ pound needed)
- 1 package reduced-fat Swiss cheese
- 1 package Canadian bacon

Grocery

- 1 small package 10-inch whole wheat tortillas

Produce

- 1 medium tomato
- 1 bag washed, ready-to-eat shredded lettuce
- 1 small bunch seedless red grapes

Staples

- Dijon mustard
- Reduced-fat mayonnaise

HELPFUL HINTS

- Old Bay seasoning is the basis for authentic Maryland crab cakes. If it is unavailable, use a shrimp or crab boil found in the spice section of the supermarket.

- The easiest way to chop the chives is to snip them with a scissors.

COUNTDOWN

- Preheat broiler.
- Make dessert.
- Toast English muffins.
- Make salad and melt cheese on muffins.

CRAB SALAD MELT

Sweet crab gives a fresh, new taste to an old childhood favorite—the classic tuna melt. Look for good-quality, canned jumbo lump or backfin, which is the select white meat from the crab.

2 whole wheat English muffins

3 tablespoons reduced-fat mayonnaise

3 tablespoons water

1 tablespoon Old Bay seasoning

¼ cup snipped chives

2 stalks celery, sliced (about 1 cup)

6 ounces canned, jumbo lump or backfin crab, drained

Salt and freshly ground black pepper

1 ounce reduced-fat Swiss cheese, sliced or shredded

Preheat broiler or toaster oven. Split English muffins in half and toast. While muffins are toasting, mix mayonnaise, water, Old Bay seasoning, and chives together in a medium-size bowl. Add the celery and crab. Mix well. Add salt and pepper to taste. Spoon crab salad onto muffins halves. Place cheese over the crab and return to the broiler. Heat just until cheese melts.

Makes 2 servings

PER SERVING: 330 calories (32 percent from fat), 11.7 g fat (2.8 g saturated, 2.6 g monounsaturated), 81 mg cholesterol, 26.7 g protein, 30.2 g carbohydrates, 4.9 g fiber, 900 mg sodium

Dessert

2 medium pears, cored and cut into cubes

Divide pear cubes between 2 dessert bowls.

Makes 2 servings

PER SERVING: 98 calories (6 percent from fat), 0.7 g fat (0 g saturated, 0 g monounsaturated), 0 mg cholesterol, 0.7 g protein, 25.1 g carbohydrates, 4.1 g fiber, 1 mg sodium

SHOPPING LIST

Seafood

- 1 can (6 ounces) jumbo lump or backfin crab

Deli

- 1 small package reduced-fat Swiss cheese

Grocery

- 1 package whole wheat English muffins
- 1 small container Old Bay Seasoning

Produce

- 1 small bunch chives
- 1 small bunch celery
- 2 medium pears

Staples

- Reduced-fat mayonnaise
- Salt
- Black peppercorns

CREAMY LETTUCE SOUP • MIXED MELON SALAD

With its delicate, nutty flavor, this soup is thick and creamy without the addition of cream. The secret is to cook the onions until they are sweet. The onions combine with the milk to form a naturally thick texture.

2 teaspoons canola oil

2 cups sliced onion

1 tablespoon all-purpose flour

1 small head romaine lettuce, sliced (about 8 cups)

1½ cups skim milk

Salt and freshly ground black pepper

¼ pound lean ham, coarsely chopped

2 tablespoons broken walnuts

2 slices whole grain bread

Heat canola oil in a large saucepan over medium heat and add the onions. Cook 5 minutes, or until onions are soft and clear but not brown. Remove pan from the heat and add the flour. Mix well. Add the lettuce and toss well until lettuce starts to wilt.

Return the pan to the heat and slowly add the milk, stirring constantly. Bring to a simmer. Do not boil. Simmer, partially covered, 10 minutes. Pour into a food processor or blender, or use a handheld blender, and process to a coarse texture. Add salt and pepper to taste. Divide between 2 large soup bowls. Sprinkle ham and walnuts on top. Serve with bread.

Makes 2 servings

PER SERVING: 414 calories (31 percent from fat), 14.5 g fat (2.6 g saturated, 6.0 g monounsaturated), 34 mg cholesterol, 27.4 g protein, 47.3 g carbohydrates, 8.6 g fiber, 925 mg sodium

Mixed Melon Salad

1 cup cubed cantaloupe

1 cup cubed honeydew
melon

Divide between 2 dessert bowls.

Makes 2 servings

PER SERVING: 58 calories (4 percent from fat), 0.2 g fat (0.1 g saturated, 0 g monounsaturated), 0 mg cholesterol, 1.1 g protein, 14.7 g carbohydrates, 1.3 g fiber, 22 mg sodium

SHOPPING LIST

Deli

● ¼ pound lean ham

Grocery

● 1 small package broken walnuts

Produce

● 1 small head romaine lettuce

● 1 cantaloupe

● 1 honeydew melon

Staples

● Onion

● All-purpose flour

● Canola oil

● Skim milk

● Whole grain bread

● Salt

● Black peppercorns

CURRIED EGG SALAD SANDWICH

The flavors of India, and curry in particular, have become very popular. Curry is a mixture of many spices that are blended together right before use. Just a touch in this egg salad sandwich lends great flavor and beautiful color. Look for curry powder in the spice section of the supermarket and use it within 6 months.

6 large eggs (only 2 yolks used)

2 tablespoons reduced-fat mayonnaise

2 tablespoons water

1½ teaspoons mild curry powder

1 celery stalk, thinly sliced (½ cup)

2 tablespoons raisins

Salt and freshly ground black pepper

4 slices whole wheat bread

1 medium tomato, sliced

Place eggs in a small saucepan and cover with cold water. Heat over medium-high heat and bring to a boil. Reduce the heat to low and gently simmer for 12 minutes. Drain pan and refill with cold water. When the eggs are cool to the touch, peel and cut in half. Discard the yolks from 4 eggs.

Mix the mayonnaise and water together until smooth. Add the curry powder. Add the celery and raisins. Toss well. Coarsely chop the egg whites and egg yolks (this can be done with a knife or mash them with a fork). Add eggs to the mayonnaise mixture. Add salt and pepper to taste. Toss gently to combine.

Toast whole wheat bread. Spread egg salad on 2 slices. Cover with tomato slices and top with remaining 2 bread slices.

Makes 2 servings

PER SERVING: 350 calories (33 percent from fat), 12.8 g fat (2.9 g saturated, 4.4 g monounsaturated), 218 mg cholesterol, 20.2 g protein, 41.0 g carbohydrates, 6.5 g fiber, 521 mg sodium

Dessert

1 cup fat-free, low-sugar
tropical fruit yogurt

Divide between 2 dessert dishes.

Makes 2 servings

PER SERVING: 69 calories (3 percent from fat), 0.2 g fat
(0.1 g saturated, 0.1 g monounsaturated), 3 mg cholesterol,
7.0 g protein, 9.4 g carbohydrates, 0 g fiber, 95 mg sodium

SHOPPING LIST

Dairy

- 1 8-ounce carton fat-free,
  low-sugar tropical fruit
  yogurt

Grocery

- 1 small container mild
  curry powder
- 1 small container raisins

Produce

- 1 small bunch celery
- 1 medium tomato

Staples

- Eggs (6 needed)
- Reduced-fat mayonnaise
- Whole wheat bread
- Salt
- Black peppercorns

HELPFUL HINT

- Ask for the roast beef to be cut in 1 large slice rather than thinly sliced. It can then be cut into cubes.

COUNTDOWN

- Preheat oven or toaster oven to 350 degrees.
- Start soup.
- While soup simmers, warm rolls.
- Finish soup.

GOULASH SOUP • CINNAMON GRAPEFRUIT

Hungarian paprika is the secret to a good goulash soup. It comes in hot or mild and can be found in the spice section of most supermarkets. Using deli roast beef, frozen chopped onion, and sliced mushrooms, you can make this soup in 15 minutes.

Goulash Soup

1 teaspoon olive oil

1 cup chopped frozen onions

2 medium garlic cloves, crushed

1 cup sliced button mushrooms

1 tablespoon Hungarian paprika

2 cups no-salt-added, chopped, canned tomatoes

1 cup water

2 whole wheat rolls (3 ounces)

1 cup sliced sweet pimientos

Salt and freshly ground black pepper

¼ pound lean deli roast beef, cut into ½-inch cubes

2 tablespoons reduced-fat sour cream

Preheat oven or toaster oven to 350 degrees. Heat olive oil in a large saucepan. Add the onion, garlic, and mushrooms. Cook 3 minutes until vegetables soften. Sprinkle the paprika over the vegetables and toss well. Add the chopped tomatoes and water. Bring to a boil, lower the heat, and simmer 10 minutes.

Put rolls in the oven to warm. Add the pimientos and salt and pepper to taste to the soup. Stir 30 seconds. Remove from heat and stir in roast beef. Serve in large soup bowls and place a spoonful of sour cream on top of each. Serve with warm rolls.

Makes 2 servings

PER SERVING: 374 calories (26 percent from fat), 11 g fat (3.6 g saturated, 3.0 g monounsaturated), 52 mg cholesterol, 26.5 g protein, 47.9 g carbohydrates, 9.6 g fiber, 308 mg sodium

Cinnamon Grapefruit

1 pink grapefruit

1 teaspoon ground
  cinnamon

Cut grapefruit in half and cut around segments.
Sprinkle cinnamon on top. Serve on 2 dessert
plates.

Makes 2 servings

PER SERVING: 41 calories (3 percent from fat), 0.1 g fat (0 g
saturated, 0 g monounsaturated), 0 mg cholesterol, 0.5 g
protein, 10.0 g carbohydrates, 0.7 g fiber, 2 mg sodium

SHOPPING LIST

Deli
- Lean deli roast beef, cut
  in 1 large slice (4 ounces)

Dairy
- 1 carton reduced-fat sour
  cream

Grocery
- 1 bag frozen chopped or
  diced onion
- 1 container Hungarian
  paprika
- 1 large can no-salt-
  added, chopped
  tomatoes
- 1 jar sliced sweet
  pimientos
- 2 whole wheat rolls

Produce
- 1 pink grapefruit
- 1 small package sliced
  button mushrooms

Staples
- Olive oil
- Garlic
- Salt
- Black peppercorns
- Cinnamon

HELPFUL HINTS

- Any type of lettuce can be substituted for this salad.

- A quick way to defrost frozen lima beans is to place them in a sieve and run hot water over them.

COUNTDOWN

- Defrost lima beans.
- Prepare ingredients.
- Assemble salad.

SHOPPING LIST

Dairy

- 1 package crumbled Roquefort cheese

Meat

- 1 package cooked, boneless, skinless chicken breast strips (4 ounces needed)

Grocery

- 1 small package frozen baby lima beans

- 1 small package whole wheat or whole grain croutons

Produce

- 1 small head frisee lettuce

- 1 medium pear

Staples

- Reduced-fat oil and vinegar dressing

FRISEE, PEAR, AND ROQUEFORT SALAD

This French salad calls for a French frisee lettuce. In America, it's called curly chicory or sometimes even curly endive. Frisee has an opened, flattened shape and curly leaves that radiate from the center like the spokes of a wheel. They are pale, almost yellow in the center, and gradually turn a dark green at the tips.

Look for a small head. The leaves are sweeter. If you find a large head, use the small, tender leaves in the middle.

4 cups packed frisee lettuce

1 medium pear, cored and sliced (about 1 cup)

¼ pound cooked, boneless, skinless chicken breast strips

2 ounces crumbled Roquefort cheese (about ½ cup)

1 cup frozen baby lima beans, thawed

1 ounce whole wheat or whole grain croutons (about ¾ cup)

2 tablespoons reduced-fat oil and vinegar dressing

Divide frisee lettuce, pear slices, and chicken strips between 2 plates or large, shallow bowls. Sprinkle Roquefort cheese, lima beans, and croutons on top. Drizzle dressing over salad. Toss well.

Makes 2 servings

PER SERVING: 418 calories (27 percent from fat), 12.6 g fat (6.0 g saturated, 0.5 g monounsaturated), 61 mg cholesterol, 33.4 g protein, 45.1 g carbohydrates, 9.1 g fiber, 640 mg sodium

GREEK BEAN AND VEGETABLE SOUP (FASSOULADA)

Known in Greece as Fassoulada, this hearty, thick soup is popular nationwide. Navy beans, onion, tomatoes, and garlic make up the basis of the soup.

1 teaspoon olive oil

1 cup frozen chopped or diced onion

1 pound zucchini, sliced (about 2 cups)

1 stalk celery, sliced (about ½ cup)

2 medium cloves garlic, crushed

2 cups fat-free, low-sodium chicken broth

1 cup no-salt-added, rinsed and drained navy beans or Great Northern beans

1 cup drained, canned, no-salt-added whole tomatoes

4 cups washed, ready-to-eat spinach

½ teaspoon dried thyme

Salt and freshly ground black pepper

¼ cup crumbled feta cheese

Heat oil in a large saucepan over medium-high heat. Add onion, zucchini, celery, and garlic. Cook 2 to 3 minutes until vegetables soften. Add chicken broth, beans, and tomatoes. Break up the tomatoes with the edge of a cooking spoon. Bring soup to a simmer and cook 5 minutes. Add the spinach and thyme. Cook until the spinach is wilted, about 1 minute. Add salt and pepper to taste. Serve in two bowls and sprinkle feta cheese on top.

Makes 2 servings

PER SERVING: 339 calories (19 percent from fat), 7.3 g fat (3.4 g saturated, 2.6 g monounsaturated), 17 mg cholesterol, 20.7 g protein, 52.6 g carbohydrates, 12.9 g fiber, 901 mg sodium

This meal contains 339 calories with 19 percent of calories from fat.

HELPFUL HINTS

- Sliced celery and carrots can be found in the produce section or on salad bars of many supermarkets. Use them to save prep time.

COUNTDOWN

- Prepare ingredients.
- Make soup.

SHOPPING LIST

Dairy

- 1 small package crumbled feta cheese

Grocery

- 1 small package frozen chopped/diced onion
- 1 small can no-salt-added whole tomatoes
- 1 small can no-salt-added navy beans or Great Northern beans
- 1 small container dried thyme

Produce

- 1 pound zucchini
- 1 small bunch celery
- 1 package washed, ready-to-eat spinach

Staples

- Olive oil
- Garlic
- Fat-free, low-sodium chicken broth
- Salt
- Black peppercorns

HELPFUL HINTS

- Any type of lettuce can be used.
- Buy ready-to-eat shredded carrots in the produce section of the market.
- Crumbled Gorgonzola cheese is available in many supermarkets. Or, buy a small amount of cheese and flake it with a fork.

COUNTDOWN

- Prepare honeydew.
- Make the wrap.

HAM AND GORGONZOLA WRAP

Tangy Gorgonzola cheese and ham are the perfect combination in this quick and flavorful sandwich. Shredded carrots add an unexpected, sweet surprise. You can make this lunch a day ahead. Wrap it in foil and refrigerate until needed. Bring to room temperature before serving.

Ham and Gorgonzola Wrap

1 tablespoon reduced-fat mayonnaise

1 tablespoon fat-free plain yogurt

½ ounce crumbled Gorgonzola cheese (about 2 tablespoons)

1 tablespoon warm water

2 10-inch whole wheat tortillas

6 ounces sliced, lean deli ham

1 cup shredded carrots

2 cups lettuce leaves

Mix mayonnaise, yogurt, Gorgonzola cheese, and water together in a small bowl. Place tortillas on a countertop and spread the cheese mixture over both. Place ham on the tortillas. Sprinkle carrots evenly over the ham. Place lettuce leaves over the carrots. Fold in the ends and roll up each tortilla lengthwise to make the wrap. Cut in half.

Makes 2 servings

PER SERVING: 347 calories (31 percent from fat), 12.0 g fat (4.1 g saturated, 2.9 g monounsaturated), 54 mg cholesterol, 25.3 g protein, 33.6 g carbohydrates, 6.0 g fiber, 1,461 mg sodium

Dessert

2 cups honeydew cubes

Divide between 2 dessert bowls.

Makes 2 servings

PER SERVING: 62 calories (3 percent from fat), 0.2 g fat (0 g saturated, 0 g monounsaturated), 0 mg cholesterol, 0.8 g protein, 16.3 g carbohydrates, 1.1 g fiber, 18 mg sodium

SHOPPING LIST

Dairy

- 1 small package crumbled Gorgonzola cheese
- 1 small carton fat-free plain yogurt

Deli

- Lean deli ham (6 ounces needed)

Grocery

- 1 package 10-inch whole wheat tortillas

Produce

- 1 bag shredded carrots
- 1 small head lettuce
- 1 container honeydew cubes

Staples

- Reduced-fat mayonnaise

HELPFUL HINTS

- If whole wheat bread crumbs are not available, process 2 slices of whole wheat bread in the food processor to make crumbs.

- Use a casserole dish or small pie plate that measures about 6 to 7 inches in diameter.

COUNTDOWN

- Preheat oven.
- Prepare ingredients.
- Make quiche.

HAM AND WILD MUSHROOM QUICHE

Homemade quiche is a perfect weekend lunch for two or 20. This 20-minute version saves time (and calories) by using bread crumbs instead of pastry dough. Best of all, it tastes just as satisfying.

Olive oil spray
½ cup whole wheat bread crumbs
4 ounces lean deli ham, torn into bite-size pieces (about 1 cup)
1 cup sliced shiitake mushrooms
1 cup sliced red onion
2 large eggs
4 egg whites
¼ teaspoon ground nutmeg
Salt and freshly ground black pepper
¼ cup reduced-fat, shredded sharp Cheddar cheese

Preheat oven to 400 degrees. Coat bottom and sides of a 6-inch shallow pie plate or casserole dish with olive oil spray. Sprinkle bread crumbs over bottom and sides of plate, rolling the plate to make sure the sides are covered. Gently shake the plate to evenly distribute excess crumbs across the bottom.

Place the ham, mushrooms, and onion in the pie plate. In a small bowl, lightly beat the 2 whole eggs and 4 egg whites with a fork. Add the nutmeg and salt and pepper to taste. Pour into the prepared pie plate. Press the ingredients under the eggs with a fork. Sprinkle cheese on top. Bake for 20 minutes. Remove, cut in half, and serve.

Makes 2 servings

PER SERVING: 381 calories (29 percent from fat), 12.5 g fat (3.9 g saturated, 4.4 g monounsaturated), 246 mg cholesterol, 33.7 g protein, 31.8 g carbohydrates, 2.2 g fiber, 1,077 mg sodium

Dessert

2 medium pears

Makes 2 servings

PER SERVING: 98 calories (6 percent from fat), 0.7 g fat (0 g saturated, 0 g monounsaturated), 0 mg cholesterol, 0.7 g protein, 25.1 g carbohydrates, 4.1 g fiber, 1 mg sodium

SHOPPING LIST

Dairy
- 1 small package reduced-fat, shredded sharp Cheddar cheese

Deli
- Lean deli ham (¼ pound needed)

Grocery
- 1 small container whole wheat bread crumbs

Produce
- 1 small package shiitake mushrooms
- 2 medium pears

Staples
- Eggs (6 needed)
- Olive oil spray
- Red onion
- Ground nutmeg
- Salt
- Black peppercorns

HELPFUL HINTS

- Honeydew melon that is already cut into cubes is available in most produce departments. Cantaloupe can be used instead.
- Ask the deli to cut the ham in one large slice. It is easier to cut into cubes this way.

COUNTDOWN

- Prepare ingredients.
- Assemble salad.

HAM, MELON, AND ENDIVE SALAD • FRUITED JELL-O

Sweet juicy honeydew melon is a delightful surprise in this salad. When shopping for Belgian endive, look for small, cigar-shaped lettuce with very pale green and cream colored, tightly packed leaves. The head only needs to be wiped with a damp paper towel. If soaked in water, the leaves will turn brown.

Ham, Melon, and Endive Salad

¼ cup fat-free plain yogurt

2 tablespoons mayonnaise

1 tablespoon Dijon mustard

2 small heads Belgian endive

6 ounces lean deli ham, cut into ½-inch cubes (about ¾ cup)

2 cups ½-inch honeydew melon cubes

1 cup diced red bell pepper

Salt and freshly ground black pepper

2 slices whole grain bread

Mix the yogurt, mayonnaise, and mustard together in a medium-size bowl until smooth.

Wipe endive with a damp paper towel. Do not soak it with water. Cut about ½ inch off the base to remove the core. Slice the endive on the diagonal into 1-inch pieces. Place in bowl and add ham, melon, and red pepper. Add salt and pepper to taste. Toss well. Toast bread. Serve salad on 2 plates with toasted bread.

Makes 2 servings

PER SERVING: 358 calories (29 percent from fat), 11.6 g fat (2.7 g saturated, 4.3 g monounsaturated), 51 mg cholesterol, 25.0 g protein, 41.5 g carbohydrates, 6.8 g fiber, 1,430 mg sodium

Fruited Jell-O

2 cups sugar-free
  raspberry Jell-O
1 cup fresh raspberries

Buy ready-to-eat, sugar-free Jell-O. Serve 1 cup per person with ½ cup raspberries sprinkled on top. Or, make Jell-O according to package instructions and measure 1 cup portions before it gels. Add ½ cup raspberries to each portion.

Makes 2 servings.

PER SERVING: 38 calories (8 percent from fat), 0.4 g fat (0 g saturated, 0 g monounsaturated), 0 mg cholesterol, 1.8 g protein, 7.1 g carbohydrates, 2.9 g fiber, 45 mg sodium

SHOPPING LIST

Dairy
- 1 small carton fat-free plain yogurt

Deli
- 1 package lean deli ham (6 ounces needed)

Grocery
- 1 container sugar-free Jell-O

Produce
- 2 small heads Belgian endive
- 1 container honeydew melon cubes
- 1 red bell pepper
- 1 small container raspberries

Staples
- Whole grain bread
- Mayonnaise
- Dijon mustard
- Salt
- Black peppercorns

HELPFUL HINTS

- Cooked chicken breast or shrimp can be used instead of ham.
- Look for whole wheat pita with 85 calories per pita or 65 calories per ounce. Each pita is 1⅓ ounces.
- Fresh chopped onion and green bell pepper from the produce section or a salad bar can be used instead of frozen.

COUNTDOWN

- Preheat broiler.
- Line baking sheet with foil.
- Make pizza.

HAM, PEPPER, AND ONION PIZZA

This pizza can be made in less time than it takes to send out for one. Frozen chopped onion and peppers and presliced mushrooms mean there's no chopping and slicing.

2 6-inch whole wheat pita breads

½ cup low-fat, no-sugar-added pizza sauce

6 ounces sliced, lean deli ham, torn into bite-size pieces

½ cup reduced-fat, shredded mozzarella cheese

½ cup sliced portobello mushrooms

½ cup frozen chopped onion

½ cup frozen chopped green bell pepper

1 teaspoon dried oregano

Preheat broiler. Line a baking sheet with foil. Place pita breads on the foil. Spoon pizza sauce over bread. Place ham over sauce. Sprinkle cheese over ham. Spread mushrooms over cheese. Sprinkle onion, green bell pepper, and oregano on top. Place under broiler about 8 to 10 inches from the heat for 5 minutes, or until warmed through.

Makes 2 servings

PER SERVING: 433 calories (28 percent from fat), 13.6 g fat (5.8 g saturated, 4.7 g monounsaturated), 66 mg cholesterol, 34.5 g protein, 45.1 g carbohydrates, 6.6 g fiber, 1,749 mg sodium

Dessert

2 medium apples

Makes 2 servings

PER SERVING: 81 calories (6 percent from fat), 0.5 g fat (0.1 g saturated, 0 g monounsaturated), 0 mg cholesterol, 0.3 g protein, 20.9 g carbohydrates, 3.7 g fiber, 0 mg sodium

SHOPPING LIST

Dairy

- 1 small package reduced-fat shredded mozzarella cheese

Deli

- 1 small package lean deli ham (6 ounces needed)

Grocery

- 1 package 6-inch whole wheat pita breads
- 1 small bottle low-fat, no-sugar-added pizza sauce
- 1 small package frozen chopped onion
- 1 small package frozen chopped green bell pepper

Produce

- 1 small package sliced portobello mushrooms
- 2 medium apples

Staples

- Dried oregano

COUNTDOWN

- Marinate shrimp.
- Preheat oven or toaster
  oven to 350 degrees.
- Prepare ingredients.
- Assemble salad.

LEMON-PEPPER SHRIMP SALAD

This salad takes only minutes to assemble using peeled cooked shrimp and pre-sliced mushrooms. But that's hard to tell by taste alone. Lemon juice and cracked black pepper give this salad a refreshing and spicy touch. Cracked black pepper is available in the spice section of the supermarket.

2 tablespoons fresh
lemon juice

2 teaspoons reduced-fat
olive oil and vinegar
dressing

½ teaspoon cracked black
pepper

½ pound shelled, cooked
shrimp

4 cups washed, ready-to-
eat baby spinach leaves

1 green bell pepper,
sliced (about 1 cup)

½ cup sliced, drained sun-
dried tomatoes packed
in olive oil

2 whole wheat rolls
(3 ounces)

1 cup sliced portobello
mushrooms

Salt

Mix lemon juice, dressing, and black pepper together. Add shrimp and let marinate while you prepare the rest of the ingredients.

Preheat oven or toaster oven to 350 degrees.

Divide spinach between 2 plates. Toss with sliced bell pepper and sun-dried tomatoes.

Warm rolls in toaster oven.

Add mushrooms to shrimp and dressing. Add salt to taste. Toss well. Spoon over salad. Serve on 2 plates with warm rolls.

Makes 2 servings

PER SERVING: 356 calories (26 percent from fat), 10.3 g fat (1.5 g saturated, 3.4 g monounsaturated), 172 mg cholesterol, 32.2 g protein, 37.6 g carbohydrates, 8.2 g fiber, 629 mg sodium

Dessert

2 medium peaches

Makes 2 servings

PER SERVING: 38 calories (6 percent from fat), 0.2 g fat (0 g saturated, 0.1 g monounsaturated), 0 mg cholesterol, 0.9 g protein, 9.3 g carbohydrates, 1.4 g fiber, 0 mg sodium

Seafood

- 1 package shelled, cooked shrimp (8 ounces needed)

Grocery

- 1 small container cracked black pepper
- 1 small jar sliced sun-dried tomatoes packed in olive oil
- 2 whole wheat rolls

Produce

- 1 lemon
- 1 green bell pepper or 1 package sliced green pepper
- 1 package washed, ready-to-eat, baby spinach leaves
- 1 package sliced portobello mushrooms
- 2 medium peaches

Staples

- Reduced-fat olive oil and vinegar dressing
- Salt

MIDDLE EASTERN PLATE

This fabulous lunch can be assembled in minutes by relying on two popular dips, hummus and baba ghannouj, that are available, ready-made, in most supermarkets. Hummus is made with ground chickpeas, garlic, lemon juice, and olive oil. Baba ghannouj is a puree of charred eggplant, tahini (pureed sesame seeds), garlic, lemon juice, and olive oil.

½ cup hummus

½ cup baba ghannouj

8 green olives

½ cup washed, ready-to-eat baby carrots

½ cup sliced green bell pepper

½ cup sliced red bell pepper

½ cup celery sticks

2 6-inch whole wheat pita breads

Divide the hummus and baba ghannouj between 2 plates. Arrange the olives, carrots, bell peppers, and celery sticks on the plates. Serve with pita bread.

Makes 2 servings

PER SERVING: 368 calories (31 percent from fat), 12.5 g fat (1.5 g saturated, 4.4 g monounsaturated), 0 mg cholesterol, 13.6 g protein, 55.0 g carbohydrates, 13.0 g fiber, 863 mg sodium

Dessert

1 cup fat-free, low-sugar mango yogurt

Divide between 2 dessert bowls.

Makes 2 servings

PER SERVING: 69 calories (3 percent from fat), 0.2 g fat (0.1 g saturated, 0.1 g monounsaturated), 3 mg cholesterol, 7.0 g protein, 9.4 g carbohydrates, 0 g fiber, 95 mg sodium

SHOPPING LIST

Dairy

- 1 small carton fat-free, low-sugar mango yogurt

Deli

- 1 small container hummus
- 1 small container baba ghannouj

Grocery

- 1 small jar green olives
- 1 small package whole wheat pita breads

Produce

- 1 package washed, ready-to-eat baby carrots
- 1 small green bell pepper
- 1 small red bell pepper
- 1 package prepared celery sticks

HELPFUL HINTS

- Two small rolls can be used instead of 1 loaf of bread.
- Balsamic vinegar can be substituted for sherry wine vinegar.
- Any flavor yogurt can be used.

COUNTDOWN

- Prepare ingredients.
- Assemble sandwich.

PAN BAGNAT

This sandwich is a specialty of the Provence region of France and literally translates as "bathed bread." It can include a variety of ingredients, though olive oil, tomatoes, and tuna are the standard fillings. The sandwich can be eaten when made or assembled the night before, wrapped tightly in foil, and refrigerated.

1 whole grain, crusty French bread (6 ounces)

Olive oil spray

1½ tablespoons olive oil

1½ tablespoons sherry wine vinegar

4 ounces tuna fish packed in water, drained (about ¾ cup)

2 tablespoons capers

Salt and freshly ground black pepper

1 small tomato, thinly sliced

¼ cup thinly sliced cucumber

Several fresh basil leaves

Cut bread in half lengthwise. Coat the cut halves with olive oil spray. Mix olive oil and vinegar together in a medium-size bowl. Add tuna and flake with a fork. Add capers and salt and pepper to taste. Toss well. Place the tuna on the bottom half of the bread. Place the tomato and cucumber slices on top. Add the basil leaves. Close the bread and wrap tightly in foil. Let sit a few minutes. Cut in half before serving.

Makes 2 servings

PER SERVING: 396 calories (34 percent from fat), 14.9 g fat (2.3 g saturated, 8.9 g monounsaturated), 18 mg cholesterol, 24.1 g protein, 44.4 g carbohydrates, 7.1 g fiber, 867 mg sodium

Dessert

1 cup fat-free, low-sugar
mixed berry yogurt

Divide between 2 dessert dishes.

Makes 2 servings

PER SERVING: 69 calories (3 percent from fat), 0.2 g fat
(0.1 g saturated, 0.1 g monounsaturated), 3 mg cholesterol,
7.0 g protein, 9.4 g carbohydrates, 0 g fiber, 95 mg sodium

SHOPPING LIST

Dairy

- 1 small carton fat-free,
  low-sugar mixed berry
  yogurt

Grocery

- 1 whole grain, crusty
  French bread
- 1 small bottle sherry wine
  vinegar
- 1 small can tuna fish
  packed in water
- 1 small bottle capers

Produce

- 1 small tomato
- 1 small cucumber
- 1 small bunch fresh basil
  leaves

Staples

- Olive oil spray
- Olive oil
- Salt
- Black peppercorns

HELPFUL HINTS

- Any type of whole grain roll can be used.
- Any type of lettuce can be used.

COUNTDOWN

- Make sauce.
- Assemble sandwich.

PO' BOY SANDWICH

The Po' Boy sandwich is a New Orleans institution. Although there are many variations of this beloved sandwich made with ingredients as varied as oysters and chicken, it seems that the classic New Orleans Po' Boy is made with roast beef. The story goes that the sandwich was developed during a transit strike in 1929 to fill a poor man for a nickel. I've created a modern version that will fill you without adding extra pounds.

2 tablespoons reduced-fat mayonnaise

2 teaspoons Dijon mustard

2 teaspoons cider vinegar

1 tablespoon capers
Several drops hot-pepper sauce

1 12-inch whole grain French baguette (about 5½ ounces)

¼ pound sliced, rare deli roast beef

2 tablespoons reduced-fat, shredded sharp Cheddar cheese

1 medium tomato, sliced
Several lettuce leaves, sliced (about 1 cup)

Mix mayonnaise, mustard, vinegar, capers, and hot-pepper sauce together. Slice baguette in half lengthwise. Spread dressing on both cut sides of the bread. Place the roast beef on the bottom half and the cheese over the roast beef. Place the tomato slices over the cheese and finish with the lettuce. Close the bread with the top half and cut in half crosswise.

Makes 2 servings

PER SERVING: 386 calories (31 percent from fat), 13.4 g fat (3.4 g saturated, 3.0 g monounsaturated), 53 mg cholesterol, 27.3 g protein, 42.0 g carbohydrates, 7.1 g fiber, 800 mg sodium

Dessert

2 medium apples

Makes 2 servings

PER SERVING: 81 calories (6 percent from fat), 0.5 g fat (0.1 g saturated, 0 g monounsaturated), 0 mg cholesterol, 0.3 g protein, 20.9 g carbohydrates, 3.7 g fiber, 0 mg sodium

SHOPPING LIST

Dairy

- 1 small package reduced-fat, shredded sharp Cheddar cheese

Deli

- Sliced, rare roast beef (¼ pound needed)

Grocery

- 1 small bottle cider vinegar
- 1 small bottle capers
- 1 12-inch whole grain French baguette

Produce

- 1 medium tomato
- 1 small head lettuce
- 2 medium apples

Staples

- Reduced-fat mayonnaise
- Dijon mustard
- Hot-pepper sauce

- Sliced deli chicken breast can be used instead of bought roasted chicken breast.

- One whole wheat baguette or 2 whole wheat rolls can substitute for a sub roll.

- Any electric grill with a top and bottom, such as a waffle iron or George Foreman grill, can be used to make a panini the traditional way. Simply assemble the sandwich, and place it in the hot grill for 2 to 3 minutes, or until the crust is crisp and the cheese melted.

COUNTDOWN

- Preheat broiler.
- Line a baking sheet with foil.
- Prepare ingredients.
- Broil sandwich.

ROASTED CHICKEN AND CHEESE PANINI • PINEAPPLES AND HONEY

Warm meats, melted cheese, and a crunchy crust have made the classic Italian panini a new American favorite. The sandwich is usually made in a special press-style grill, but you can enjoy an equally delicious version with this broiler cooking method.

Roasted Chicken and Cheese Panini

1 whole wheat sub roll (about 6 ounces)

¼ pound roasted or rotisserie chicken breast, bones and skin removed (about 1¼ cups)

½ cup sliced roasted red peppers

2 ounces sliced Gruyère cheese

Several fresh basil leaves

Preheat broiler. Slice roll in half lengthwise. Place two halves top side up on foil-lined baking sheet. Broil 30 seconds to crisp bread. Remove from broiler.

Cut chicken into small strips. Turn bread over to cut side up. Place chicken on one side of bread and top with red pepper. Place cheese on other half of bread. Place in broiler and broil for 1 minute. Remove and place basil on top. Close the two halves together and press the sandwich down. Cut in half and serve.

Makes 2 servings

PER SERVING: 412 calories (30 percent from fat), 13.7 g fat (6.9 g saturated, 4.5 g monounsaturated), 71 mg cholesterol, 33.4 g protein, 41.3 g carbohydrates, 6.6 g fiber, 585 mg sodium

Pineapples and Honey

1 cup fresh pineapple
cubes

2 teaspoons honey

Divide pineapples between 2 dessert bowls.
Drizzle honey on top.

Makes 2 servings

PER SERVING: 38 calories (0 percent from fat), 0.3 g fat
(0 g saturated, 0 g monounsaturated), 0 mg cholesterol,
0.3 g protein, 9.6 g carbohydrates, 1.0 g fiber, 1 mg sodium

SHOPPING LIST

Dairy

- 1 package sliced Gruyère
  cheese

Meat

- Roasted or rotisserie
  chicken breast (4 ounces
  needed)

Grocery

- 1 whole wheat sub roll
- 1 small bottle roasted
  red peppers

Produce

- 1 small bunch fresh basil
  leaves
- 1 container fresh
  pineapple cubes

Staples

- Honey

HELPFUL HINTS

- Any flavor yogurt can be used.
- A quick way to chop parsley is to snip the leaves off the stem with a scissors.

COUNTDOWN

- Cook sausages and onion.
- Prepare remaining ingredients.
- Assemble salad.

SAUSAGE AND BEET SALAD

Colorful beets contain powerful nutrient compounds that can help protect against heart disease and certain cancers. Their texture, color, and sweet taste create a pleasing contrast with the savory sausage.

½ pound low-fat Italian turkey sausages, cut into ½-inch pieces (about 1⅓ cups)

1 cup sliced yellow onion

3 tablespoons reduced-fat oil and vinegar dressing

1 teaspoon caraway seeds

2 cups drained canned sliced beets

1 cup shredded carrots

Salt and freshly ground black pepper

½ cup chopped parsley

2 slices rye bread

Heat a nonstick skillet over medium-high heat and add the sausage slices and onions. Cook 5 minutes, or until sausage is cooked through. Meanwhile, pour dressing into a medium-size bowl. Add the caraway seeds, sliced beets, carrots, and salt and pepper to taste. Toss without breaking up the beet slices. Spoon onto 2 plates. Spoon the sausage and onion on top. Sprinkle with chopped parsley. Serve with bread.

Makes 2 servings

PER SERVING: 421 calories (30 percent from fat), 14.2 g fat (2.8 g saturated, 3.6 g monounsaturated), 84 mg cholesterol, 27.9 g protein, 45.6 g carbohydrates, 6.1 g fiber, 1,170 mg sodium

Dessert

1 cup fat-free, low-sugar, orange-flavored yogurt

Divide between 2 bowls.

Makes 2 servings

PER SERVING: 69 calories (3 percent from fat), 0.2 g fat (0.1 g saturated, 9.1 g monounsaturated), 3 mg cholesterol, 7.0 g protein, 9.4 g carbohydrates, 0 g fiber, 95 mg sodium

SHOPPING LIST

Dairy
- 1 carton fat-free, low-sugar, orange-flavored yogurt

Meat
- 1 package low-fat Italian turkey sausages (8 ounces needed)

Grocery
- 1 small container caraway seeds
- 1 can sliced beets
- Rye bread

Produce
- 1 small package shredded carrots
- 1 small bunch parsley

Staples
- Yellow onion
- Reduced-fat oil and vinegar dressing
- Salt
- Black peppercorns

HELPFUL HINTS

- Look for large, shelled, cooked shrimp in the seafood department.
- Place sardines in a sieve and carefully rinse them so that they remain whole.
- Tuna fish packed in water can be substituted for sardines.

COUNTDOWN

- Assemble ingredients.
- Arrange plate.

SEAFOOD ANTIPASTO PLATE (ANTIPASTO DI MARE)

The colorful display of antipasti dishes is a welcoming scene in many Italian restaurants. Here's an array you can quickly assemble using prepared marinated vegetables, cooked shrimp, and sardines. Sardines are an excellent source of omega-3 fatty acids essential to a balanced diet. They're also an excellent source of protein and calcium.

Several red lettuce leaves

4 ounces large, shelled, cooked shrimp

4 ounces canned sardines, rinsed and drained

½ cup canned roasted red peppers

½ cup canned marinated artichoke hearts

½ cup marinated mushrooms

4 pitted black olives

2 tablespoons lemon juice

Freshly ground black pepper

12 whole wheat breadsticks

Wash and dry lettuce leaves and line 2 plates with them. Arrange shrimp, sardines, red pepper, artichoke hearts, mushrooms, and black olives in separate sections on the plate. Sprinkle lemon juice over the shrimp and sardines. Add black pepper over the shrimp, to taste. Serve with breadsticks.

Makes 2 servings

PER SERVING: 351 calories (31 percent from fat), 12.1 g fat (1.7 g saturated, 4.1 g monounsaturated), 166 mg cholesterol, 31.0 g protein, 31.1 g carbohydrates, 5.7 g fiber, 778 mg sodium

Dessert

1 cup fat-free, low-sugar chocolate frozen yogurt

Divide between 2 dessert bowls.

Makes 2 servings

PER SERVING: 100 calories (7 percent from fat), 0.8 g fat (0.5 g saturated, 0.2 g monounsaturated), 4 mg cholesterol, 4.1 g protein, 18.3 g carbohydrates, 1.9 g fiber, 76 mg sodium

SHOPPING LIST

Dairy

- 1 small carton fat-free, low-sugar chocolate frozen yogurt

Seafood

- 1 package large, shelled, cooked shrimp (4 ounces needed)

Grocery

- 1 small can sardines
- 1 small jar roasted red peppers
- 1 small jar marinated artichoke hearts
- 1 small bottle marinated mushrooms
- 1 small container pitted black olives
- 1 package whole wheat breadsticks

Produce

- 1 small head red lettuce
- 1 large lemon

Staples

- Black peppercorns

Photo on page 54.

HELPFUL HINTS

- Ripe plums, papaya, or mangoes can be substituted for the peaches.
- Any type of short-cut pasta such as macaroni or penne can be used.
- Any flavor yogurt can be used.
- Cooked, peeled shrimp is available from the seafood department. It comes in frozen. Keep a bag in the freezer for quick meals.
- An easy way to chop chives is to snip them with a scissors.

COUNTDOWN

- Place water for pasta on to boil.
- Prepare ingredients.
- Assemble salad.

SHRIMP AND PEACH PASTA SALAD

It's a real treat when ripe, juicy peaches are in season. In this salad, they provide a contrasting sweet flavor to the tangy dressing.

Buy cooked shrimp for this salad, and the only cooking you will need to do is boil the pasta.

This lunch can be made a day ahead. Bring to room temperature before serving.

2 ounces fusilli (corkscrew) pasta (about ¾ cup)

4 tablespoons reduced-fat mayonnaise

3 tablespoons water

2 tablespoons prepared horseradish

2 tablespoons Dijon mustard

6 ounces peeled, cooked shrimp

4 cups washed, ready-to-eat salad greens

1 red bell pepper, cut into 1-inch pieces (about 1 cup)

2 ripe, medium peaches, cut into 1-inch pieces (1 rounded cup)

4 tablespoons chopped fresh chives

Place a large pot of water on to boil over high heat. Add pasta and cook 10 minutes, or according to package instructions.

Mix mayonnaise, water, horseradish, and mustard together in a medium-size bowl. Drain pasta, rinse in cold water, and drain thoroughly. Add to the bowl. Add shrimp and toss well.

Line 2 dinner plates with the salad greens. Spoon pasta and shrimp over the top. Place bell pepper slices and peaches on top. Sprinkle with chives.

Makes 2 servings

PER SERVING: 387 calories (30 percent from fat), 13.0 g fat (1.9 g saturated, 3.5 g monounsaturated), 139 mg cholesterol, 25.3 g protein, 44.4 g carbohydrates, 6.6 g fiber, 593 mg sodium

Dessert

1 cup fat-free, low-sugar
  blueberry yogurt

Divide between 2 dessert dishes.

Makes 2 servings

PER SERVING: 69 calories (3 percent from fat), 0.2 g fat (0.1 g saturated, 0.1 g monounsaturated), 3 mg cholesterol, 7.0 g protein, 9.4 g carbohydrates, 0 g fiber, 95 mg sodium

SHOPPING LIST

Dairy

- 1 small carton fat-free, low-sugar blueberry yogurt

Seafood

- 1 package peeled, cooked shrimp (6 ounces needed)

Grocery

- 1 small package fusilli (corkscrew-shaped pasta)
- 1 small bottle prepared horseradish

Produce

- 1 bag washed, ready-to-eat salad greens
- 1 red bell pepper
- 2 ripe, medium peaches
- 1 small bunch fresh chives

Staples

- Reduced-fat mayonnaise
- Dijon mustard

HELPFUL HINTS

- Any type of smoked fish can be used except smoked salmon.
- Trimmed green beans can be found in the produce section of most supermarkets, or look for them at the salad bar.

COUNTDOWN

- Assemble dessert and set aside.
- Make salad.

SMOKED TROUT SALAD • PINEAPPLE AND COCONUT FLAKES

The delicate texture and strong flavor of smoked fish contrast nicely with the crunchy, sharp, and tangy flavor of dill pickle in this intriguing salad.

Smoked Trout Salad

10 ounces washed, ready-to-eat field greens (about 8 cups)

2 cups trimmed green beans, cut into 2-inch pieces

3 tablespoons reduced-fat oil and vinegar dressing

¼ cup diced dill pickles

1 cup sliced, canned pimiento

½ pound smoked trout fillets, cut into strips

2 slices whole grain bread

Divide salad greens between 2 plates. Place the green beans in a medium-size bowl, toss with dressing, and add to the greens. Add the dill pickles and pimiento and toss the salad. Place smoked trout on top. Serve with whole grain bread.

Makes 2 servings

PER SERVING: 367 calories (32 percent from fat), 12.9 g fat (2.0 g saturated, 4.2 g monounsaturated), 64 mg cholesterol, 33.3 g protein, 33.6 g carbohydrates, 11.9 g fiber, 645 mg sodium

Pineapple and Coconut Flakes

4 slices fresh pineapple
(about 2 cups)

2 tablespoons desiccated
sweetened coconut
flakes

Divide pineapple slices between 2 dessert plates. Sprinkle coconut flakes on top.

Makes 2 servings

PER SERVING: 104 calories (19 percent from fat), 2.2 g fat (1.4 g saturated, 0.1 g monounsaturated), 0 mg cholesterol, 0.8 g protein, 22.9 g carbohydrates, 2.3 g fiber, 14 mg sodium

SHOPPING LIST

Seafood

• Smoked trout fillets (8 ounces needed)

Grocery

• 1 small can/bottle sweet pimiento

• 1 package desiccated sweetened coconut flakes

• 1 small jar dill pickles

Produce

• 1 bag washed, ready-to-eat field greens

• 1 package trimmed green beans

• 1 package fresh pineapple slices

Staples

• Whole grain bread

• Reduced-fat oil and vinegar dressing

HELPFUL HINTS

- Any type of reduced-fat oil and vinegar dressing can be used.
- Any type of canned beans can be used.
- Cooked, peeled shrimp are available from the seafood department. They come in frozen. Keep a bag in the freezer for quick meals.
- A quick way to slice scallions is to snip them with a scissors.
- If fresh lychees are unavailable, use canned or frozen. Canned lychees should be well drained and rinsed.

COUNTDOWN

- Prepare ingredients.
- Assemble salad.

SPICY ASIAN SHRIMP SALAD

Ginger and soy sauce added to a basic oil and vinegar dressing lend an Asian touch to this shrimp and black bean salad. Chopped peanuts and scallions add a finishing touch.

2 tablespoons reduced-fat oil and vinegar dressing

2 teaspoons low-sodium soy sauce

½ teaspoon ground ginger

1 cup canned, rinsed, and drained black beans

2 scallions, sliced

½ pound cooked, peeled, and deveined shrimp

Several romaine lettuce leaves

2 tablespoons chopped unsalted peanuts

2 tablespoons chopped fresh mint

Mix dressing, soy sauce, and ginger together in a medium-size bowl. Add the black beans, scallions, and shrimp. Toss well. Tear the lettuce leaves into large pieces and place on 2 plates. Divide the shrimp mixture in half and spoon over lettuce. Sprinkle peanuts and mint on top.

Makes 2 servings

PER SERVING: 348 calories (27 percent from fat), 10.3 g fat (1.4 g saturated, 3.1 g monounsaturated), 172 mg cholesterol, 34.6 g protein, 30.3 g carbohydrates, 7.2 g fiber, 560 mg sodium

Dessert

1 cup fresh lychees

Divide between 2 dessert bowls.

Makes 2 servings.

PER SERVING: 63 calories (8 percent from fat), 0.6 g fat (0.1 g saturated, 0.1 g monounsaturated), 0 mg cholesterol, 0.8 g protein, 15.7 g carbohydrates, 1.3 g fiber, 1 mg sodium

SHOPPING LIST

Seafood

- 1 package cooked, peeled, and deveined shrimp (8 ounces needed)

Grocery

- 1 small bottle low-sodium soy sauce
- 1 small container ground ginger
- 1 small can black beans
- 1 small container unsalted peanuts

Produce

- 1 small bunch scallions
- 1 small head romaine lettuce
- 1 small bunch mint
- 1 container fresh lychees

Staples

- Reduced-fat oil and vinegar dressing

Photo on page 55.

HELPFUL HINTS

- Canned jalapeño peppers can be used instead of fresh.
- Whole grain hamburger rolls can be substituted for whole wheat.

COUNTDOWN

- Assemble dessert.
- Prepare ingredients.
- Make burgers.

TEXAS TUNA BURGER WITH JALAPEÑO MAYONNAISE • BANANA AND STRAWBERRIES

These burgers get their bang from jalapeño peppers that are mixed into mayonnaise. Scallions and onion flavor fresh tuna for these juicy tuna burgers.

Texas Tuna Burgers with Jalapeño Mayonnaise

1 medium jalapeño pepper, seeded (about 1 tablespoon)

2 tablespoons reduced-fat mayonnaise

6 ounces fresh tuna, coarsely chopped

2 scallions, sliced (about ¾ cup)

¼ cup frozen chopped onion

Salt and freshly ground black pepper

Olive oil spray

2 whole wheat hamburger rolls (about 3 ounces)

1 small tomato, sliced

2 romaine lettuce leaves

Chop jalapeño peppers in a food processor fitted with a chopping blade. Remove and mix with the mayonnaise. Set aside. Without washing the food processor bowl, add the tuna, scallions, and onion and pulse several times until ingredients are finely chopped. Add salt and pepper to taste. Form into 2 patties, about 4 inches in diameter and ½ inch thick. Heat a nonstick skillet over medium-high heat and coat with olive oil spray. Add the burgers and cook 2 minutes. Turn and cook 2 minutes longer. Place each burger on the bottom half of a hamburger roll. Place several slices of tomato on each burger and lettuce leaves over the tomato. Spread the mayonnaise on the top half of the roll and close.

Makes 2 servings

PER SERVING: 298 calories (28 percent from fat), 9.3 g fat (1.6 g saturated, 2.3 g monounsaturated), 44 mg cholesterol, 26.1 g protein, 29.1 g carbohydrates, 5.6 g fiber, 384 mg sodium

Banana and Strawberries

1 medium banana,
  peeled and sliced
  (about 1¼ cups)

1 cup sliced strawberries

Divide the banana and strawberry slices between 2 dessert dishes.

Makes 2 servings

PER SERVING: 110 calories (6 percent from fat), 0.7 g fat (0.2 g saturated, 0.1 g monounsaturated), 0 mg cholesterol, 1.4 g protein, 27.7 g carbohydrates, 4.0 g fiber, 2 mg sodium

SHOPPING LIST

Seafood

- Fresh tuna (6 ounces needed)

Grocery

- 1 small package whole wheat hamburger rolls
- 1 package frozen chopped or diced onion

Produce

- 1 jalapeño pepper
- 1 small bunch scallions
- 1 small tomato
- 1 small head romaine lettuce
- 1 medium banana
- 1 small container strawberries

Staples

- Reduced-fat mayonnaise
- Olive oil spray
- Salt
- Black peppercorns

HELPFUL HINTS

- Any type of sprouts can be used.
- This lunch can be made the night before, wrapped, and refrigerated. Bring to room temperature before serving.
- Leftover cranberry sauce can be frozen for future use.

COUNTDOWN

- Assemble ingredients.
- Make wrap.

TURKEY CRANBERRY WRAP

Turkey and cranberry sauce make a great combination any time of year. Use leftover turkey slices or your favorite deli turkey for this simple wrap.

¼ cup canned cranberry sauce

2 tablespoons reduced-fat mayonnaise

2 10-inch whole wheat tortillas

6 ounces deli turkey breast, sliced

2 tablespoons broken pecan pieces

1 cup alfalfa sprouts

Mix cranberry sauce and mayonnaise together. Place tortillas on a countertop and spread cranberry mixture evenly over tortillas. Place the turkey slices over the sauce. Sprinkle pecans on top. Place alfalfa sprouts over the turkey. Fold in the ends and roll up each tortilla lengthwise to make the wrap. Cut in half.

Makes 2 servings

PER SERVING: 384 calories (31 percent from fat), 13.3 g fat (2.3 g saturated, 4.5 g monounsaturated), 59 mg cholesterol, 26.4 g protein, 39.8 g carbohydrates, 4.6 g fiber, 392 mg sodium

Dessert

4 plums

Makes 2 servings

PER SERVING: 72 calories (10 percent from fat), 0.8 g fat (0.1 g saturated, 0.1 g monounsaturated), 0 mg cholesterol, 1.0 g protein, 17.2 g carbohydrates, 2.0 g fiber, 0 mg sodium

SHOPPING LIST

Deli

- 6 ounces sliced turkey breast

Grocery

- 1 can cranberry sauce
- 1 package 10-inch whole wheat tortillas
- 1 package pecan pieces

Produce

- 1 package alfalfa sprouts
- 4 plums

Staples

- Reduced-fat mayonnaise

HELPFUL HINTS

- Any type of firm, country-style bread can be used. If it is too fresh, toast it for a few minutes.

- Cooked, boneless, skinless chicken breast strips are available in most supermarkets. If difficult to find, use store-bought rotisserie chicken breasts and remove the skin and bones.

- To shave Parmesan cheese, bring it to room temperature and use a potato peeler to make thin strips.

COUNTDOWN

- Assemble dessert.
- Prepare the salad ingredients.
- Add the dressing.

TUSCAN TOMATO AND BREAD SALAD • ORANGE AND PINE NUT SLICES

The rolling green hills of Tuscany provided the setting where I first tasted this classic Tuscan salad, known by its Italian name, Panzanella. "Tuscan women don't waste a crust of bread," my Italian friend told me. The base of the salad is moistened stale bread, which is mixed with fresh basil, chopped ripe tomatoes, minced red onion, and dressing. The addition of chicken makes it a complete meal.

Tuscan Tomato and Bread Salad

2 slices whole grain bread (1 to 2 days old)

1 medium tomato, coarsely chopped (about 1 cup)

1 packed cup fresh basil leaves

1 cup arugula

½ medium cucumber, peeled and coarsely chopped (about 1 cup)

6 pitted black olives, cut in half

Salt and freshly ground black pepper

2 tablespoons reduced-fat olive oil and vinegar dressing

½ pound cooked, boneless, skinless chicken breast strips (about 1 cup)

1 ounce shaved Parmesan cheese (about ½ cup)

Soak the bread for a few seconds in a small bowl of water. When just soft, squeeze out all of the water and break into small pieces. Place bread in a bowl with tomato, basil, arugula, cucumber, and olives. Add salt and pepper to taste. Add dressing and mix well. Divide between 2 dinner plates. Divide chicken and Parmesan over the top.

Makes 2 servings

PER SERVING: 322 calories (27 percent from fat), 9.7 g fat (3.0 g saturated, 2.9 g monounsaturated), 80 mg cholesterol, 38.4 g protein, 20.6 g carbohydrates, 4.6 g fiber, 631 mg sodium

Orange and Pine Nut Slices

2 tablespoons pine nuts

2 medium oranges,
   peeled and sliced

Place pine nuts on a tray and toast in a toaster oven about 30 seconds, or until golden. Or place in a small skillet and cook over medium heat. Divide orange slices between 2 dessert plates and sprinkle pine nuts on top.

Makes 2 servings

PER SERVING: 111 calories (37 percent from fat), 4.5 g fat (0.7 g saturated, 1.7 g monounsaturated), 0 mg cholesterol, 3.3 g protein, 16.7 g carbohydrates, 3.5 g fiber, 0 mg sodium

SHOPPING LIST

Dairy

- 1 small package Parmesan cheese

Meat

- 1 package cooked, boneless, skinless chicken breast strips (8 ounces needed)

Grocery

- 1 small jar pitted black olives
- 1 small package pine nuts

Produce

- 1 medium tomato
- 1 small bunch basil
- 1 small bunch arugula
- 1 medium cucumber
- 2 medium oranges

Staples

- Whole grain bread
- Reduced-fat olive oil and vinegar dressing
- Salt
- Black peppercorns

HELPFUL HINTS

- Any type of rotisserie or cooked, boneless, skinless chicken breast can be used.
- Any flavor of fat-free, low-sugar yogurt can be used.
- Use the pulse button on the food processor to coarsely chop the apple, walnuts, and celery.

COUNTDOWN

- Assemble ingredients.
- Make wrap.

WALDORF WRAP

Crunchy Waldorf salad made with apples, walnuts, and celery is an American classic. The addition of cooked chicken strips and a soft whole wheat tortilla to hold everything together turn this classic into a quick and tasty wrap.

1½ tablespoons reduced-fat mayonnaise

1 tablespoon lemon juice
   Salt and freshly ground black pepper

2 tablespoons broken walnut pieces

1 small red apple, cored and cut into quarters (about 1 cup)

1 celery stalk, sliced (about ½ cup)

2 10-inch whole wheat tortillas

¼ pound cooked, boneless, skinless chicken strips

Mix mayonnaise and lemon juice together in a medium-size bowl. Add salt and pepper to taste. Coarsely chop the walnuts, apple quarters, and celery in a food processor or by hand. Add to the bowl. Toss well. Place tortillas on a countertop and spread the apple mixture evenly over them. Place the chicken strips on top. Fold in the ends and roll up each tortilla lengthwise to make the wrap. Cut them in half and place on two plates.

Makes 2 servings

PER SERVING: 336 calories (32 percent from fat), 12.1 g fat (2.1 g saturated, 2.0 g monounsaturated), 44 mg cholesterol, 21.8 g protein, 35.4 g carbohydrates, 5.7 g fiber, 380 mg sodium

Dessert

1 cup fat-free, low-sugar, coffee-flavored yogurt

Divide between 2 dessert bowls.

Makes 2 servings

PER SERVING: 69 calories (3 percent from fat), 0.2 g fat (0.1 g saturated, 0.1 g monounsaturated), 3 mg cholesterol, 7.0 g protein, 9.4 g carbohydrates, 0 g fiber, 95 mg sodium

SHOPPING LIST

Dairy

- 1 small carton fat-free, low-sugar coffee-flavored yogurt.

Meat

- Cooked, boneless, skinless chicken breast, cut into strips (¼ pound needed)

Grocery

- 1 small package walnut pieces
- 1 small package 10-inch whole wheat tortillas

Produce

- 1 lemon
- 1 small red apple
- 1 small bunch celery

Staples

- Reduced-fat mayonnaise
- Salt
- Black peppercorns

DINNER

All the healthful, nutritionally balanced dinners in this chapter are quick and easy. The Helpful Hints and Countdown show you substitutions and preparation shortcuts to help you get your dinner on the table without having to think—a no-brainer approach. The average calorie count for the dinners, including the dessert suggestions, is 643 with 26 percent of calories from fat. Like all the recipes in this book, the dinner menus emphasize fruits, vegetables, whole grains, and lean protein, and are low in saturated fats, trans fats, cholesterol, sodium, and added sugars.

SEAFOOD

Cajun-Bronzed Mahi Mahi • Rice and Spinach Pilaf 130

Catfish with Mango Chutney • Black Bean and Rice Salad 132

Crab Scampi and Spaghetti 134

Greek Lemon Fish • Cracked Wheat Salad (Tabbouleh) 136

Halibut in Cider • Saffron Rice 138

Julia's Simple Salmon • Gratineed Cauliflower 140

Salmon Gazpacho • Rice Salad 142

Shrimp Quesadilla • Chipotle Corn Salad 144

Sicilian Swordfish with Broccoli Linguine 146

HELPFUL HINTS

- Any type of firm fish such as grouper, snapper, U.S. farmed catfish, or tilapia can be used.

- Cajun spice mixes can be found in the spice section of the super-market.

- An electric frying pan can be used instead of a skillet. Keep the temperature at 350 degrees.

- The general rule for cooking fish is 10 minutes for a 1-inch-thick piece. If the fish is thicker or thinner, adjust the cooking time using the 10-minute rule as a guideline. Remember, the fish will continue to cook after it is removed from the heat. I usually cook the fish 8 minutes per inch to account for this.

COUNTDOWN

- Start rice.
- Make fish.
- Finish rice.

CAJUN-BRONZED MAHI MAHI • RICE AND SPINACH PILAF

Unlike the popular "blackening" technique used to cook Cajun-style fish, this mahi mahi achieves a beautiful golden color, along with incredible flavor, from the bronzing cooking method.

Paul Prudhomme, one of America's favorite chefs and considered the father of blackened redfish, had this to say: "My advice to people at home is bronzing rather than blackening. This avoids the smoke and the risk of handling a red-hot skillet while still achieving an excellent result."

The secret to bronzing is to keep the skillet at the right temperature. The fish should take 6 to 9 minutes to cook. If it takes much longer, the skillet is not hot enough.

Use the Cajun spice mixture given in the recipe or use 1 tablespoon prepared Cajun spice seasoning mix, available in most supermarkets.

Dessert Suggestion: Fruit Compote (page 193) goes well with this meal.

Cajun-Bronzed Mahi Mahi

¼ teaspoon cayenne pepper

½ teaspoon garlic powder

1 teaspoon dried oregano

1 teaspoon dried thyme

¾ pound mahi mahi fillet

2 teaspoons olive oil

Mix cayenne pepper, garlic powder, oregano, and thyme together. Spoon half of spice mixture onto one side of the fish, pressing it into the flesh. Heat a skillet over high heat and add the oil. When it is very hot, add the mahi mahi, seasoned side down. Spread remaining spice mixture on top side of the fish. Cook until the underside is bronze in color, 3 to 4 minutes. Cook second side 3 to 4 minutes, or until cooked through. The fish is ready when a knife inserted into the flesh shows opaque rather than translucent meat.

Makes 2 servings

PER SERVING: 193 calories (27 percent from fat), 508 g fat (1.0 g saturated, 3.5 g monounsaturated), 126 mg cholesterol, 31.7 g protein, 1.6 g carbohydrates, 0.7 g fiber, 151 mg sodium

Rice and Spinach Pilaf

1 teaspoon olive oil

1 cup 10-minute brown rice

1 cup low-sodium tomato juice

4 cups washed, ready-to-eat spinach

Salt and freshly ground black pepper

Heat olive oil in a large nonstick skillet over medium-high heat. Add rice and cook 1 minute. Add tomato juice. Bring to a simmer, lower heat, cover, and simmer 5 minutes. Remove from heat and stir in the spinach. Cover and let stand 5 minutes. Add salt and pepper to taste. Fluff with a fork before serving.

Makes 2 servings

PER SERVING: 226 calories (16 percent from fat), 3.9 g fat (0.6 g saturated, 2.2 g monounsaturated), 0 mg cholesterol, 6.3 g protein, 43.0 g carbohydrates, 4.2 g fiber, 63 mg sodium

SHOPPING LIST

Seafood

- Mahi mahi fillet (¾ pound needed)

Grocery

- 1 small container cayenne pepper
- 1 small container dried thyme
- 1 can low-sodium tomato juice

Produce

- 1 bag washed, ready-to-eat spinach

Staples

- Garlic powder
- Dried oregano
- Olive oil
- 10-minute brown rice
- Salt
- Black peppercorns

HELPFUL HINTS

- Mango chutney is available in most supermarkets. Look for one that has 50 calories per tablespoon, no fat, and 13 grams carbohydrates.

- Any type of canned beans can be substituted for black beans.

- If catfish is not available, use snapper, sole, or grouper.

- A quick way to chop cilantro is to snip the leaves with a scissors right off the stem.

- The general rule for cooking fish is 10 minutes for a 1-inch-thick piece. If the fish is thicker or thinner, adjust the cooking time using the 10-minute rule as a guideline. Remember, the fish will continue to cook after it is removed from the heat. I usually cook the fish 8 minutes per inch to account for this.

COUNTDOWN

- Start rice.
- Make fish.
- Finish rice.

CATFISH WITH MANGO CHUTNEY • BLACK BEAN AND RICE SALAD

Catfish is now farm-raised in the United States and has a mild flavor and firm texture. It's a good seafood choice, doesn't contribute to depleting ocean populations, and its quality is consistent. Mango chutney adds a sweet and savory topping.

Dessert Suggestion: Mocha-Cream Cake (page 197) goes well with this meal.

Catfish with Mango Chutney

2 teaspoons canola oil
¾ pound catfish fillets
Salt and freshly ground black pepper
2 tablespoons mango chutney

Heat the oil in a nonstick skillet over medium-high heat and add fish fillets. Cook 5 minutes, turn, and cook 4 minutes for a fish that is 1 inch thick. Sprinkle cooked side with salt and pepper to taste. Remove fish from skillet, add mango chutney, and heat for 30 seconds until warm. Spoon chutney on top of fish and serve.

Makes 2 servings

PER SERVING: 234 calories (23 percent from fat), 6.0 g fat (1.4 g saturated, 4.0 g monounsaturated), 83 mg cholesterol, 31.7 g protein, 12.0 g carbohydrates, 0.2 g fiber, 60 mg sodium

Black Bean and Rice Salad

1 cup water

1 cup 10-minute brown rice

½ cup rinsed and drained canned black beans

1 cup cilantro, chopped

4 tablespoons reduced-fat oil and vinegar dressing

Salt and freshly ground black pepper

Several red lettuce leaves

1 medium tomato, sliced

Bring water to a boil in a large saucepan over high heat. Stir in rice, return to a boil, reduce heat to medium, cover, and simmer 5 minutes. Remove from heat and let stand, covered, 5 minutes. Add black beans, cilantro, 3 tablespoons dressing, and salt and pepper to taste. Fluff with a fork. Serve on top of lettuce leaves with sliced tomato on the side. Drizzle remaining dressing over tomatoes.

Makes 2 servings

PER SERVING: 310 calories (18 percent from fat), 6.3 g fat (0.8 g saturated, 0.6 g monounsaturated), 0 mg cholesterol, 9.7 g protein, 54.6 g carbohydrates, 6.8 g fiber, 245 mg sodium

SHOPPING LIST

Seafood

- Farm-raised catfish fillets (¾ pound needed)

Grocery

- 1 bottle mango chutney
- 1 can black beans

Produce

- 1 bunch cilantro
- 1 small head red lettuce
- 1 medium tomato

Staples

- Canola oil
- 10-minute brown rice
- Reduced-fat oil and vinegar dressing
- Salt
- Black peppercorns

This meal contains 554 calories with 19 percent of calories from fat.

Photo on page 56.

HELPFUL HINTS

- Look for jumbo lump canned or frozen crab. Backfin crab can be substituted.

- This recipe will also work with imitation crabmeat.

- The quickest way to chop parsley and basil is to snip the leaves with a scissors.

COUNTDOWN

- Place water for spaghetti on to boil.

- Make scampi.

- Cook spaghetti.

CRAB SCAMPI AND SPAGHETTI

To Italians, scampi is a small lobster called a prawn. However, in the United States, scampi has become a term for the sauce that goes with seafood. Jumbo lump crab in a garlic-wine sauce is a new take on this traditional Italian dish.

Open a bag of Italian-style washed, ready-to-eat lettuce to complete the meal.

Crab Scampi

2   teaspoons olive oil

3   cloves garlic, crushed

¾   cup dry vermouth

1   tablespoon Worcestershire sauce

Several drops hot-pepper sauce

¾   pound canned or frozen jumbo lump crabmeat

½   cup fresh parsley, chopped

Salt and freshly ground black pepper

Heat olive oil in a nonstick skillet over medium-high heat and add garlic, vermouth, Worcestershire sauce, and hot-pepper sauce. Cook 1 minute to blend flavors. Add crab and toss for 1 minute to warm crab. Sprinkle with parsley and salt and pepper to taste.

Makes 2 servings

PER SERVING: 303 calories (19 percent from fat), 6.5 g fat (1.0 g saturated, 3.7 g monounsaturated), 132 mg cholesterol, 31.5 g protein, 4.8 g carbohydrates, 0.7 g fiber, 598 mg sodium

Spaghetti

¼ pound whole wheat thin spaghetti

2 teaspoons olive oil

Salt and freshly ground black pepper

Bring a large saucepan with 3 to 4 quarts water to a boil over high heat. Add spaghetti and boil 8 to 9 minutes. Remove 2 tablespoons cooking water and reserve. Drain spaghetti and place back in saucepan with reserved water and olive oil. Toss well. Add salt and pepper to taste. Toss and serve topped with Crab Scampi.

Makes 2 servings

PER SERVING: 251 calories (19 percent from fat), 5.4 g fat (0.7 g saturated, 3.4 g monounsaturated), 0 mg cholesterol, 7.3 g protein, 42.6 g carbohydrates, 1.4 g fiber, 4 mg sodium

SHOPPING LIST

Seafood

- 1 can or package jumbo lump crabmeat (12 ounces needed)

Grocery

- 1 small bottle dry vermouth
- 1 small bottle Worcestershire sauce
- 1 package whole wheat thin spaghetti

Produce

- 1 small bunch parsley

Staples

- Olive oil
- Garlic
- Hot-pepper sauce
- Salt
- Black peppercorns

HELPFUL HINT

- A quick way to chop parsley and mint and to slice scallions is to snip them with a scissors.

COUNTDOWN

- Soak bulgur wheat.
- Prepare remaining ingredients.
- Make fish.
- Finish salad.

GREEK LEMON FISH • CRACKED WHEAT SALAD (TABBOULEH)

Lemon juice, olive oil, fresh mint, and parsley are sunny flavors reminiscent of the lush, sun-drenched, rolling hills in Greece where these products grow in abundance.

Bulgur wheat, used in the Cracked Wheat Salad, is made by steaming, drying, and crushing wheat kernels. A secret to flavoring bulgur wheat in this recipe is to squeeze the scallions and wheat together so that the juices from the scallions penetrate the wheat.

The general rule for cooking fish is 10 minutes for a 1-inch-thick piece. If the fish is thicker or thinner, adjust the cooking time using the 10-minute rule as a guideline. Remember, the fish will continue to cook after it is removed from the heat. I usually cook the fish 8 minutes per inch to account for this.

Dessert Suggestion: Melon with Ouzo (page 196) goes well with this meal.

Greek Lemon Fish

1½ tablespoons lemon juice

1 tablespoon olive oil

1 teaspoon dried oregano

Olive oil spray

¾ pound fish fillets (snapper, flounder, tilapia, sole, striped bass, U.S. farmed catfish)

Salt and freshly ground black pepper

Whisk lemon juice, olive oil, and oregano together. Set aside. Heat a nonstick skillet over medium-high heat. Coat with olive oil spray and add fish fillets. Cook 2 minutes. Turn and cook 2 minutes for a ½-inch fillet (cook 4 minutes per side for a 1-inch fillet). Add salt and pepper to taste. Divide between 2 dinner plates and spoon sauce from the pan over top.

Makes 2 servings

PER SERVING: 247 calories (39 percent from fat), 10.6 g fat (1.6 g saturated, 5.4 g monounsaturated), 60 mg cholesterol, 35.0 g protein, 1.2 g carbohydrates, 0.4 g fiber, 108 mg sodium

Cracked Wheat Salad (Tabbouleh)

⅔ cup uncooked fine bulgur wheat

4 scallions, sliced (about 1½ cups)

½ cup chopped flat parsley

½ cup chopped fresh mint

3 tablespoons reduced-fat olive oil and vinegar dressing

Salt and freshly ground black pepper

2 cups grape or cherry tomatoes

Place bulgur wheat in a medium-size bowl and add warm water to cover. Let stand 20 minutes. Drain in a fine sieve and squeeze out as much moisture as possible with your hands. Return bulgur to the bowl and add the scallions, squeezing mixture again to combine flavors. Add parsley, mint, and dressing and toss well. Add salt and pepper to taste. Spoon onto plate and place tomatoes on top.

Makes 2 servings

PER SERVING: 261 calories (16 percent from fat), 4.6 g fat (0.5 g saturated, 0.2 g monounsaturated), 0 mg cholesterol, 9.4 g protein, 50.8 g carbohydrates, 13.5 g fiber, 209 mg sodium

SHOPPING LIST

Seafood

- Fish fillets such as snapper, flounder, tilapia, sole, striped bass, U.S. farmed catfish (¾ pound needed)

Grocery

- Uncooked fine bulgur wheat

Produce

- 1 bunch scallions
- 1 bunch parsley
- 1 bunch mint
- 1 small package grape or cherry tomatoes
- 2 lemons

Staples

- Olive oil
- Dried oregano
- Olive oil spray
- Reduced-fat olive oil and vinegar dressing
- Salt
- Black peppercorns

Photo on page 57 and back cover.

HELPFUL HINTS

- Cod or haddock can be used instead of halibut.

- Turmeric can be used instead of saffron for the rice.

- Hard cider is available in the liquor department of many supermarkets. If you can't find it, use sweet cider, light beer, or apple juice in the recipe.

- A quick way to chop parsley is to snip the leaves off the stem with a scissors.

COUNTDOWN

- Start rice.
- Make halibut.
- Complete rice.

HALIBUT IN CIDER • SAFFRON RICE

This delightful dish is from the Asturias region of northern Spain, located on the northern coast of the Iberian Peninsula, which is famous for its hard cider. Before fermentation, apple cider is called "sweet." If allowed to ferment, the cider becomes hard. The alcohol content can vary.

Hake is the traditional fish used for this Spanish meal. It can be difficult to find in the United States, so I have used halibut instead in this recipe.

The general rule for cooking fish is 10 minutes for a 1-inch-thick piece. If the fish is thicker or thinner, adjust the cooking time using the 10-minute rule as a guideline. Remember, the fish will continue to cook after it is removed from the heat. I usually cook the fish 8 minutes per inch to account for this.

Halibut in Cider

¼ cup all-purpose flour
  Salt and freshly ground black pepper
¾ pound halibut
2 teaspoons olive oil
3 medium cloves garlic, crushed
2 medium tomatoes, cut into 1-inch pieces (about 2 cups)
¾ cup hard cider

Place flour on a plate and add salt and pepper to taste. Roll halibut in the flour, making sure all sides are coated. Shake off excess. Heat olive oil in a medium-size nonstick skillet over medium-high heat. Add halibut and brown 3 minutes, turn, and brown second side 2 minutes. Remove to a plate. Sprinkle with salt and pepper to taste. Raise heat and add garlic, tomatoes, and cider to the skillet. Cook 5 minutes to thicken sauce. If tomatoes are watery, cook a few more minutes. Return fish to skillet, lower heat, and cook in sauce 3 minutes. Remove fish to 2 dinner plates and spoon sauce over fish.

Makes 2 servings

PER SERVING: 399 calories (20 percent from fat), 9.0 g fat (1.3 g saturated, 4.7 g monounsaturated), 54 mg cholesterol, 39.1 g protein, 28.5 g carbohydrates, 3.0 g fiber, 111 mg sodium

Saffron Rice

2 teaspoons olive oil

1 cup 10-minute brown rice

1 cup water

⅛ teaspoon saffron

Salt and freshly ground black pepper

¼ cup chopped fresh parsley

Heat olive oil in a medium-size nonstick skillet over medium heat. Add rice and toss 1 minute. Add water and saffron. Bring to a simmer and cover. Simmer 5 minutes. Remove from heat and let stand, covered, 5 minutes. Add salt and pepper to taste. Fluff with a fork and sprinkle parsley on top. Serve with halibut.

Makes 2 servings

PER SERVING: 209 calories (21 percent from fat), 4.8 g fat (0.7 g saturated, 3.4 g monounsaturated), 0 mg cholesterol, 3.3 g protein, 37.0 g carbohydrates, 0.6 g fiber, 2 mg sodium

SHOPPING LIST

Seafood

- Halibut (¾ pound needed)

Grocery

- 1 bottle hard cider
- 1 small package saffron

Produce

- 2 medium tomatoes
- 1 bunch parsley

Staples

- All-purpose flour
- Olive oil
- Garlic
- 10-minute brown rice
- Salt
- Black peppercorns

JULIA'S SIMPLE SALMON • GRATINEED CAULIFLOWER

Julia Child lives on in the hearts of many Americans because of her profound influence on their cooking. In an interview with her on my NPR radio program, I asked her what she cooked for herself when she was home. "I love to cook and I love to eat and I like my own cooking. I get very depressed if I don't eat nicely. I have fun with whatever I'm cooking," was her answer. Broiled salmon with a gratin of fresh cauliflower was inspired by her trip to the local farmer's market in Santa Barbara, California.

"I cook things that are easy and perfectly simple ... not something covered with a lot of goo. That way, you can tell what it is and it tastes good," she told me. When she saw a beautiful, white cauliflower in the market, she decided to just steam it, add cheese, and place it under the broiler to brown. She suggested a green salad to go with this easy dinner.

I have adapted this recipe in fond remembrance of our relationship.

Dessert Suggestion: Very Berry Crepes (page 202) go well with this meal.

Julia's Simple Salmon

Olive oil spray

¾ pound salmon fillet

2 tablespoons fresh dill or 1 teaspoon dried

Salt and freshly ground black pepper

½ small crusty whole grain or whole wheat baguette

Line a baking tray with foil and place under the broiler while other ingredients are prepared. Remove baking tray from oven and coat with olive oil spray. Place salmon on baking tray and coat with olive oil spray. Broil about 6 inches from the heat for 10 minutes. Remove to individual dinner plates and sprinkle with dill and salt and pepper to taste. Place bread on bottom shelf of oven for the last 2 minutes to warm through.

Makes 2 servings

PER SERVING: 350 calories (34 percent from fat), 13.3 g fat (2.1 g saturated, 4.3 g monounsaturated), 96 mg cholesterol, 37.8 g protein, 19.4 g carbohydrates, 2.9 g fiber, 294 mg sodium

Gratineed Cauliflower

4 cups cauliflower florets

¼ cup plain bread crumbs

¼ cup reduced-fat, shredded sharp Cheddar cheese

2 teaspoons olive oil

Salt and freshly ground black pepper

Cut large florets in half and place in a vegetable steamer over boiling water. Steam 5 minutes. Or place in a microwaveable dish without water and microwave, covered, on high for 5 minutes. Arrange the florets in a casserole dish with heads turned up. Mix bread crumbs, cheese, and olive oil together. Toss with salt and pepper to taste. Sprinkle over the top of the cauliflower and place under the broiler for 3 minutes, or until the cheese becomes slightly brown.

Makes 2 servings

PER SERVING: 168 calories (36 percent from fat), 6.6 g fat (1.5 g saturated, 4.0 g monounsaturated), 3 mg cholesterol, 9.1 g protein, 20.5 g carbohydrates, 5.3 g fiber, 263 mg sodium

SHOPPING LIST

Dairy

- 1 small package reduced-fat, shredded sharp Cheddar cheese

Seafood

- Salmon fillet (¾ pound needed)

Grocery

- 1 small crusty whole grain or whole wheat baguette
- 1 small container plain bread crumbs

Produce

- 1 small bunch fresh dill or 1 jar dried dill
- 1 package cauliflower florets

Staples

- Olive oil spray
- Olive oil
- Salt
- Black peppercorns

HELPFUL HINTS

- Salmon fillets or steak can be used.

- The general rule for cooking fish is 10 minutes for a 1-inch-thick piece. If the fish is thicker or thinner, adjust the cooking time using the 10-minute rule as a guideline. Remember, the fish will continue to cook after it is removed from the heat. I usually cook the fish 8 minutes per inch to account for this.

COUNTDOWN

- Prepare ingredients.
- Cook salmon.
- Toast bread.
- Make rice.
- Complete soup.

SALMON GAZPACHO • RICE SALAD

Fresh salmon, cucumbers, and tomatoes make a soothing soup supper. Gazpacho is a Spanish soup dish traditionally served at room temperature or chilled. Adding freshly cooked salmon creates an entree where the soup ingredients flavor the salmon. A quick vegetable rice completes the dinner.

The secret to the rich flavor of this dinner is that the salmon is cooked for just a few minutes on its own and removed from the saucepan, so that it does not overcook. It's then added to the remaining soup ingredients.

The salmon may be a little red in the center when it is removed from the skillet. It will continue to cook in its own heat once it is removed.

Dessert Suggestion: Spiced Oranges (page 199) go well with this meal.

Salmon Gazpacho

¾ pound salmon fillet
1 cup low-sodium tomato juice
1 cup diced ripe tomatoes
¼ cup diced Vidalia or red onion
¼ cup + 2 tablespoons diced cucumber, divided use
2 teaspoons olive oil
2 teaspoons balsamic vinegar
1 cup nonfat, plain yogurt
Salt and freshly ground black pepper
2 slices crusty whole grain country bread
2 scallions sliced (about ½ cup)

Heat a nonstick skillet over medium-high heat. Add the salmon and cook 3 minutes. Turn and cook 3 minutes longer for a ¾-inch piece. If the salmon is thicker, cook another 2 minutes per side, until salmon is cooked through.

While salmon cooks, divide the tomato juice, tomatoes, onion, ¼ cup cucumber, olive oil, balsamic vinegar, and yogurt between the 2 soup bowls. Stir to blend. Add salt and pepper to taste. Toast bread. When cool enough to handle, cut cooked salmon into 1- to 2-inch pieces and divide between the bowls. Scatter scallions and the remaining 2 tablespoons diced cucumber on top. Serve with toasted bread.

Makes 2 servings

PER SERVING: 473 calories (32 percent from fat), 17.1 g fat (2.7 g saturated, 7.5 g monounsaturated), 99 mg cholesterol, 46.0 g protein, 35.3 g carbohydrates, 5.0 g fiber, 337 mg sodium

Rice Salad

¼ cup quick-cooking
brown rice

½ cup water

1 cup drained sliced
roasted red pepper

2 tablespoons reduced-
fat olive oil and vinegar
dressing

Salt and freshly ground
black pepper

Place rice and water in a small saucepan. Bring to a boil, lower heat, and simmer 10 minutes. Or cook according to package instructions. Drain and place in a serving bowl. Add red pepper, salad dressing, and salt and pepper to taste. Toss well.

Makes 2 servings.

PER SERVING: 132 calories (21 percent from fat), 3.1 g fat (0.4 g saturated, 0.3 g monounsaturated), 0 mg cholesterol, 2.7 g protein, 23.9 g carbohydrates, 2.5 g fiber, 117 mg sodium.

SHOPPING LIST

Dairy

- 1 small carton nonfat, plain yogurt

Seafood

- Salmon fillet (¾ pound needed)

Grocery

- 1 small can low-sodium tomato juice
- 1 small loaf crusty, whole grain country bread
- 1 small bottle roasted red peppers

Produce

- 1 medium tomato
- 1 medium cucumber
- 1 small bunch scallions

Staples

- Olive oil
- Vidalia or red onion
- Balsamic vinegar
- Reduced-fat olive oil and vingar dressing
- Quick-cooking brown rice
- Salt
- Black peppercorns

HELPFUL HINTS

- Fruit salsa or other types of salsas can be used instead of tomato salsa.
- Any type of Mexican-style cheese can be used.
- Use 2 skillets to speed cooking time.
- If you prefer a fiery dressing, add a chopped chipotle pepper to the mayonnaise along with the adobo sauce.

COUNTDOWN

- Preheat broiler.
- Assemble salad.
- Make quesadillas.

SHRIMP QUESADILLA • CHIPOTLE CORN SALAD

This quesadilla is a hot sandwich—Tex-Mex style. It's filled with juicy shrimp, cheese, and salsa and makes a quick Southwestern dinner.

Chipotle peppers lend a smoky flavor to the salad. Chipotle peppers are a red jalapeño chile pepper that is ripened, dried, and smoked. They're sold dried or canned in adobo sauce. Make the salad recipe here—or, for a quicker salad, open a bag of washed, ready-to-eat salad and serve with oil and vinegar dressing to which you have added a teaspoon of chopped chipotle pepper.

Shrimp Quesadilla

½ **pound peeled, deveined, cooked shrimp**

Olive oil spray

4 **8-inch whole wheat tortillas**

½ **cup tomato salsa**

1 **cup reduced-fat, shredded Monterey Jack cheese, divided use**

Preheat broiler. Slice shrimp in half lengthwise, from tail to head end. Heat a nonstick skillet over medium heat. Coat with olive oil spray. Place 1 tortilla in skillet. Spread half the salsa on the tortilla. Arrange half the shrimp on the salsa. Set aside ¼ cup shredded cheese. Place half the remaining ¾ cup cheese over the shrimp. Cover with a second tortilla and with a lid. Cook 2 minutes. Remove lid and place 2 tablespoons of the reserved cheese on top of the tortilla. Place the skillet under the broiler for 1 minute. Remove skillet from oven and transfer the quesadilla to a plate with a spatula. Cut into wedges. Repeat for second quesadilla.

Makes 2 servings

PER SERVING: 475 calories (30 percent from fat), 15.9 g fat (8.5 g saturated, 0.3 g monounsaturated), 202 mg cholesterol, 42.8 g protein, 35.9 g carbohydrates, 5.0 g fiber, 1,189 mg sodium

Chipotle Corn Salad

2 cups washed, ready-to-eat shredded lettuce

2 tablespoons reduced-fat mayonnaise

1 teaspoon adobo sauce from canned chipotle pepper

2 tablespoons warm water

1 cup frozen corn kernels, defrosted (1 minute in microwave oven)

1 cup chopped red bell pepper

Place shredded lettuce on a plate. Mix mayonnaise, adobo sauce, and water together. Spoon corn and red bell pepper over the lettuce. Spoon sauce over salad.

Makes 2 servings

PER SERVING: 146 calories (35 percent from fat), 5.7 g fat (0.9 g saturated, 1.5 g monounsaturated), 5 mg cholesterol, 4.0 g protein, 23.7 g carbohydrates, 4.6 g fiber, 151 mg sodium

SHOPPING LIST

Dairy

- 1 small package reduced-fat, shredded Monterey Jack cheese

Seafood

- 1 package peeled, deveined, cooked shrimp (8 ounces needed)

Grocery

- 1 package 8-inch whole wheat tortillas
- 1 small jar tomato salsa
- 1 small can chipotle pepper in adobo sauce
- 1 package frozen corn kernels

Produce

- 1 bag washed, ready-to-eat shredded lettuce
- 1 medium red bell pepper

Staples

- Olive oil spray
- Reduced-fat mayonnaise

SICILIAN SWORDFISH WITH BROCCOLI LINGUINE

Tomatoes, olives, and garlic are well-known staples for zesty Sicilian cooking. However, the raisins in this dish are actually another common ingredient in many traditional Italian dishes. They lend a sweet contrast to the acidic flavor of tomatoes.

Dessert Suggestion: Creamy Balsamic Strawberries (page 192) go well with this meal.

Sicilian Swordfish

1 cup canned, low-sodium, diced tomatoes

3 cloves garlic, crushed

5 pitted black olives

2 tablespoons raisins

1 tablespoon fresh oregano or 1 teaspoon dried

Salt and freshly ground black pepper

1 teaspoon olive oil

¾ pound swordfish (about ¾ inch thick)

FOR THE SAUCE:

Microwave method: Place tomatoes, garlic, olives, raisins, and oregano in a microwaveable bowl. Cover with a paper towel and microwave on high 3 minutes. Add salt and pepper to taste.

Stove-top method: Place tomatoes and garlic in a small saucepan over medium heat and simmer 5 minutes. Add olives, raisins, and oregano and continue to cook 5 minutes. Add salt and pepper to taste.

FOR FISH:

Heat olive oil in a small nonstick skillet over medium-high heat. Add swordfish. Brown for 2 minutes on each side. Salt and pepper the cooked sides. Lower heat to medium and continue to cook 2 minutes, or until fish is cooked. It will look opaque inside, not translucent. Remove from skillet and divide into 2 equal portions. Serve over linguine (see recipe on opposite page) and spoon sauce over top.

Makes 2 servings

PER SERVING: 288 calories (32 percent from fat), 10.4 g fat (2.4 g saturated, 5.3 g monounsaturated), 66 mg cholesterol, 35.2 g protein, 13.3 g carbohydrates, 2.4 g fiber, 258 mg sodium

Broccoli Linguine

¼ pound fresh or dry linguine

½ pound broccoli florets (about 3 cups)

¼ cup reserved boiling pasta liquid

1 teaspoon olive oil

Salt and freshly ground black pepper

Bring a large pot with 3 quarts of water to a boil over high heat. Add linguine. Cook 2 minutes if using fresh pasta or 9 minutes (or according to package directions) if using dried. Add broccoli in the last 2 minutes of cooking. Remove ¼ cup water from pot and drain linguine and broccoli. Mix olive oil into reserved water. Pour over linguine and broccoli and toss. Add salt and pepper to taste. Place on individual plates. Arrange fish over pasta and spoon sauce on top.

Makes 2 servings

PER SERVING: 269 calories (12 percent from fat), 3.6 g fat (0.5 g saturated, 1.8 g monounsaturated), 0 mg cholesterol, 11.2 g protein, 49.5 g carbohydrates, 5.3 g fiber, 40 mg sodium

SHOPPING LIST

Seafood
- Swordfish (¾ pound needed)

Grocery
- 1 can low-sodium, diced tomatoes
- 1 small container pitted black olives
- 1 small package raisins
- 1 small package fresh linguine

Produce
- 1 small bunch fresh oregano (or 1 container dried oregano)
- ½ pound broccoli florets

Staples
- Olive oil
- Garlic
- Salt
- Black peppercorns

POULTRY

Brazilian-Style Chicken with Quinoa 150

Chicken Satay with Thai Peanut Sauce • Broccoli and Rice 152

Crispy Chicken • Provencal Vegetables (Ratatouille) 154

Curry-Kissed Chicken • Carrots and Rice 156

Italian Meat Loaf • Hot Pepper Lentils 158

Jacques Pepin's Mediterranean Chicken over Spinach • Garlic Beans 160

Mexican Orange Chicken • Green Pepper Rice 162

Poached Chicken with Fresh Tomato-Mayonnaise Sauce • Rice Salad 164

Southwestern Chicken Burgers • Quick Slaw 166

Turkey Skillet Casserole • Tossed Salad 168

Wasabi Chicken • Pan-Roasted Corn and Broccoli 170

HELPFUL HINTS

- Brown rice can be
  substituted if quinoa is
  not available.

- If fresh okra is not
  available year-round in
  your grocery store,
  frozen okra can be used
  instead.

- Chicken breasts with
  bone in and wing
  removed can be found in
  most supermarkets. If
  not, remove wing and
  skin from chicken breast
  before using in this
  recipe.

COUNTDOWN

- Start chicken.
- While chicken cooks,
  make quinoa.

BRAZILIAN-STYLE CHICKEN WITH QUINOA

Ginger, cumin, cayenne pepper, and coconut milk are some of the diverse flavors commonly found in many Brazilian dishes. In this particular meal, these intriguing ingredients are coupled with quinoa, an ancient grain indigenous to the Andes Mountains in South America. It's quick for a weeknight meal or special enough for the weekend and guests.

Dessert Suggestion: Plum Meringue (page 192) goes well with this meal.

Brazilian-Style Chicken

1 teaspoon ground
    ginger

2 teaspoons ground
    cumin

¼ teaspoon cayenne
    pepper

2 chicken breast halves,
    bone in, wings and skin
    removed, about
    ½ pound each

2 teaspoons canola oil

1 cup sliced onion

1 clove garlic, crushed

½ cup fat-free, low-
    sodium chicken broth

½ pound okra, trimmed
    and sliced (about
    2 cups)

½ cup light coconut milk
    Salt and freshly ground
    black pepper

2 tablespoons dry-
    roasted peanuts,
    coarsely chopped

Mix ginger, cumin, and cayenne pepper together and rub over chicken. Heat oil in a large nonstick skillet over medium-high heat and brown chicken on all sides, about 5 minutes. Add onion and garlic and continue to cook 1 minute. Add chicken broth and okra. Bring to a simmer. Lower heat to medium, cover, and simmer 15 minutes, until chicken is no longer pink inside and a meat thermometer inserted in the thickest portion registers 170 degrees. Add coconut milk and stir into sauce. Add salt and pepper to taste. Scatter peanuts on top. Serve over Quinoa (see recipe on opposite page).

Makes 2 servings

PER SERVING: 408 calories (36 percent from fat), 16.2 g fat (3.9 g saturated, 7.1 g monounsaturated), 96 mg cholesterol, 46.7 g protein, 22.4 g carbohydrates, 5.6 g fiber, 372 mg sodium

Quinoa

½ cup quinoa

1½ cups water

　Salt and freshly ground black pepper

In a fine mesh sieve, rinse quinoa under cold water. Drain. Place quinoa and water in a saucepan. Season to taste with salt and pepper. Bring to a boil over high heat. Cover with a lid and cook 10 minutes. All of the water should be absorbed. If the pan runs dry before the quinoa is cooked, add more water. Place quinoa on a plate and serve chicken, vegetables, and sauce on top.

Makes 2 servings

PER SERVING: 159 calories (14 percent from fat), 2.5 g fat (0.3 g saturated, 0.7 g monounsaturated), 0 mg cholesterol, 5.6 g protein, 29.3 g carbohydrates, 2.5 g fiber, 9 mg sodium

SHOPPING LIST

Meat

- Chicken breasts bone in (16 ounces needed)

Grocery

- 1 small container ground ginger
- 1 small container ground cumin
- 1 small container cayenne pepper
- 1 small jar dry-roasted peanuts
- 1 can light coconut milk
- 1 box quinoa

Produce

- ½ pound okra

Staples

- Canola oil
- Onion
- Garlic
- Fat-free, low-sodium chicken broth
- Salt
- Black peppercorns

HELPFUL HINT

- Rice vinegar can be bought in the Asian section of the supermarket. A half tablespoon water mixed with a half tablespoon distilled white vinegar may be used as a substitute.

COUNTDOWN

- Preheat broiler and baking tray.
- Start rice.
- While rice cooks, prepare remaining ingredients.
- Make peanut sauce.
- Broil chicken satay.

CHICKEN SATAY WITH THAI PEANUT SAUCE • BROCCOLI AND RICE

These skewers of seafood or meat are usually served alongside a spicy peanut sauce.

Use this easy sauce recipe or buy a thick, bottled peanut sauce to use instead. The sauce here is mildly spicy, so if you like it hot, add more hot-pepper sauce.

If using wooden skewers, be sure to soak them in water for about 30 minutes before use. This keeps them from burning on the grill or under the broiler.

Dessert Suggestion: Lemon-Lime Pineapple Slices (page 195) go well with this meal.

Chicken Satay with Thai Peanut Sauce

¾ pound boneless, skinless chicken breast, cut into 4 long strips (approximately ½ inch thick and 4 inches long)

4 8-inch wooden or metal skewers

Olive oil spray

Salt and freshly ground black pepper

Salt and freshly ground black pepper

FOR THE THAI PEANUT SAUCE:

2 tablespoons crunchy peanut butter

2 tablespoons low-sodium soy sauce

1 tablespoon rice vinegar

6 drops hot-pepper sauce

1 teaspoon cornstarch

2 tablespoons water

Move an oven rack so that it is about 4 inches from the heat. Preheat broiler. Line a baking tray with foil and place under broiler to heat. Thread the chicken strips onto the skewers. (I find that threading in a wave pattern allows more even cooking.) Remove baking sheet from oven and coat with olive oil spray. Place skewers on sheet. Coat chicken with olive oil spray. Sprinkle with salt and pepper to taste. Place under broiler for 3 minutes. Divide the skewers between 2 dinner plates.

TO MAKE THE THAI PEANUT SAUCE

Mix peanut butter, soy sauce, and vinegar together in a microwaveable bowl until blended with a smooth consistency. Add hot-pepper sauce. Mix cornstarch and water together and blend into the mixture. Microwave on high 1 minute or cook in a saucepan over medium heat until sauce is thick, about 2 minutes. If sauce becomes too thick, add another tablespoon of water to make it a thick-pouring consistency. Spoon the sauce over the chicken.

Makes 2 servings

PER SERVING: 315 calories (35 percent from fat), 12.3 g fat (2.4 g saturated, 4.3 g monounsaturated), 96 mg cholesterol, 43.9 g protein, 6.5 g carbohydrates, 1.1 g fiber, 719 mg sodium

Broccoli and Rice

1 cup water

1 cup 10-minute brown rice

¼ pound broccoli florets (about 1½ cups)

2 teaspoons canola oil

Salt and freshly ground black pepper

Place water in a medium-size saucepan and bring to a boil over high heat. Add the rice and broccoli, cover with a lid, and simmer 5 minutes. Remove from the heat and let stand, covered, 5 minutes. Add the canola oil and salt and pepper to taste. Toss well.

Makes 2 servings

PER SERVING: 230 calories (24 percent from fat), 6.1 g fat (0.9 g saturated, 3.8 g monounsaturated), 0 mg cholesterol, 5.6 g protein, 39.2 g carbohydrates, 3.6 g fiber, 21 mg sodium

SHOPPING LIST

Meat

- Boneless, skinless chicken breast (¾ pound needed)

Grocery

- 1 small jar crunchy peanut butter
- 1 small bottle low-sodium soy sauce
- 1 small bottle rice vinegar

Produce

- ¼ pound broccoli florets

Staples

- Olive oil spray
- Canola oil
- Hot-pepper sauce
- Cornstarch
- 10-minute brown rice
- Salt
- Black peppercorns

CRISPY CHICKEN • PROVENCAL VEGETABLES (RATATOUILLE)

This tasty blend of Provencal vegetables and crispy, sautéed chicken makes a quick, colorful dinner. Coating the chicken with coarse cornmeal gives it a flavorful crust without having to deep-fry it. Cornmeal can be found in three textures—coarse, medium, and fine—and three colors—white, yellow, and blue, depending on the type of corn used. White and yellow cornmeal can be found in most supermarkets.

Complete this Provencal meal with some crusty, whole meal country bread.

Dessert Suggestion: Velvety Chocolate Mousse (page 201) goes well with this meal.

Crispy Chicken

¼ cup coarse cornmeal

Salt and freshly ground black pepper

1 egg white

¾ pound boneless, skinless chicken thighs

2 teaspoons olive oil

Put cornmeal in a bowl and season with salt and pepper to taste. In another bowl, lightly beat the egg white. Dip chicken thighs into egg white and then cornmeal mixture, making sure both sides are well coated. Heat olive oil in a nonstick skillet over medium-high heat. Add chicken and cook for 5 minutes. Turn and cook 4 minutes longer, until juices run clear. A meat thermometer inserted in the thickest portion should read 180 degrees.

Makes 2 servings

PER SERVING: 316 calories (47 percent from fat), 11.3 g fat (2.3 g saturated, 5.4 g monounsaturated), 138 mg cholesterol, 37.4 g protein, 13.6 g carbohydrates, 1.3 g fiber, 147 mg sodium

Provencal Vegetables (Ratatouille)

½ pound eggplant, washed, unpeeled, and sliced (about 3 cups)

½ pound zucchini, washed and sliced (about 2 cups)

¼ pound sliced button mushrooms (about 1⅔ cups)

1½ cups low-fat, low-sodium pasta sauce

Salt and freshly ground black pepper

2 slices multigrain bread

Add eggplant, zucchini, mushrooms, and pasta sauce to a medium-size saucepan. Bring to a simmer over medium heat. Lower heat and cover. Simmer 15 minutes. Vegetables should be cooked through but a little firm. Add salt and pepper to taste. Serve with bread.

Makes 2 servings

PER SERVING: 214 calories (6 percent from fat), 1.5 g fat (0.3 g saturated, 0.4 g monounsaturated), 0 mg cholesterol, 11.2 g protein, 43.9 g carbohydrates, 11.1 g fiber, 690 mg sodium

SHOPPING LIST

Meat

- Boneless, skinless chicken thighs (¾ pound needed)

Grocery

- 1 small bottle low-fat, low-sodium pasta sauce
- 1 small package coarse cornmeal

Produce

- ½ pound eggplant
- ½ pound zucchini
- 1 package sliced button mushrooms

Staples

- Egg
- Olive oil
- Multigrain bread
- Salt
- Black peppercorns

Photo on page 58.

HELPFUL HINT

- If chicken tenders are not available, use boneless, skinless chicken breast and cut them into 3-inch strips.

COUNTDOWN

- Place water for rice on to boil.
- Assemble ingredients for chicken.
- Cook rice.
- While rice cooks, make chicken.

CURRY-KISSED CHICKEN • CARROTS AND RICE

A dusting of curry flavors this simple chicken dish. With ready-to-eat shredded carrots, found in the produce section of most supermarkets, there's no slicing or dicing for this easy meal. Just add them to the rice right after it is cooked, and they'll warm through but lend a crisp texture.

The curry powder sold in supermarkets is a blend of about 15 herbs, spices, and seeds. This type of powder loses its flavor quickly. If you have curry powder that is more than six months old, buy a new one. It will add more flavors to the dish.

Curry-Kissed Chicken

1½ tablespoons curry powder
¾ pound chicken tenders
Olive oil spray
Salt and freshly ground black pepper
⅓ cup water
3 tablespoons apricot jam
¼ cup heavy whipping cream
2 tablespoons scallions

Place curry powder on a plate. Toss the chicken tenders in the curry powder, making sure all sides are coated. Heat a nonstick skillet over medium-high heat and coat with olive oil spray. Add the chicken tenders and cook 2 minutes per side, until no longer pink inside. Add salt and pepper to taste. Remove to a clean plate. Add the water and apricot jam to the skillet and simmer 30 seconds, stirring to melt jam. Add cream and simmer 1 minute to thicken sauce. Add salt and pepper to taste. Spoon sauce over chicken. Scatter scallions on top.

Makes 2 servings

PER SERVING: 392 calories (35 percent from fat), 15.3 g fat (7.7 g saturated, 4.0 g monounsaturated), 137 mg cholesterol, 40.7 g protein, 23.2 g carbohydrates, 2.1 g fiber, 135 mg sodium

Carrots and Rice

1 cup water

1 cup 10-minute brown rice

½ cup shredded carrots

2 teaspoons olive oil

Salt and freshly ground black pepper

Bring water to a boil in a large saucepan. Stir in rice, return to a boil, reduce heat to medium, cover, and simmer 5 minutes. Remove from heat and stir in shredded carrots. Cover and let stand 5 minutes. Add oil and salt and pepper to taste. Fluff with a fork.

Makes 2 servings

PER SERVING: 224 calories (24 percent from fat), 5.9 g fat (0.9 g saturated, 3.8 g monounsaturated), 0 mg cholesterol, 4.0 g protein, 38.8 g carbohydrates, 2.6 g fiber, 14 mg sodium

SHOPPING LIST

Dairy
- 1 small carton heavy whipping cream

Meat
- Chicken tenders (¾ pound needed)

Grocery
- 1 small jar apricot jam
- 1 small container curry powder

Produce
- 1 bag shredded carrots
- 1 small bunch scallions

Staples
- 10-minute brown rice
- Olive oil
- Olive oil spray
- Salt
- Black peppercorns

HELPFUL HINT

- The lentils take time to cook, so start them first and let them cook while you prepare the meat loaf.

COUNTDOWN

- Preheat oven to 400 degrees.
- Make lentils.
- Prepare meat loaf.

ITALIAN MEAT LOAF • HOT PEPPER LENTILS

Meat loaf, well-seasoned and served with a tomato-mushroom sauce, makes a delicious entree. Adding a side dish of spicy lentils completes the meal. Be sure the package says white meat turkey only. It's available in most supermarkets.

Lentils are rich in minerals and contain more protein than dried beans. I like them because they don't need soaking and cook in about 30 minutes.

Italian Meat Loaf

Olive oil spray

¾ pound 99% fat-free ground white meat turkey

1 teaspoon fennel seeds

2 tablespoons plain bread crumbs

½ cup chopped or diced frozen onion

2 medium cloves garlic, crushed

2 tablespoons balsamic vinegar

Salt and freshly ground black pepper

1 egg, lightly beaten

½ cup sliced mushrooms

½ cup low-fat, low-sodium pasta sauce

Preheat oven to 400 degrees. Line a baking sheet with foil and coat with olive oil spray.

Mix ground turkey, fennel seeds, bread crumbs, onion, garlic, and balsamic vinegar together. Add salt and pepper to taste. Add the egg to the turkey mixture and gently stir until ingredients blend together. Shape into 2 loaves about 5 inches by 3 inches and place on baking sheet. Spread mushrooms and pasta sauce on top. Bake 15 minutes, or until cooked through. A meat thermometer should read 170 degrees.

Makes 2 servings

PER SERVING: 311 calories (12 percent from fat), 4.2 g fat (1.2 g saturated, 1.2 g monounsaturated), 215 mg cholesterol, 48.6 g protein, 18.8 g carbohydrates, 2.9 g fiber, 361 mg sodium

Hot Pepper Lentils

1 cup fat-free, low-sodium chicken broth

1 cup water

½ cup chopped or diced frozen onion

⅛ teaspoon crushed red-pepper flakes

½ cup dried lentils

1 tablespoon olive oil

2 teaspoons dried oregano

Salt and freshly ground black pepper

Bring chicken broth and water to a boil over high heat in a medium-size saucepan. Add onion and red-pepper flakes. Rinse lentils in a strainer and remove any foreign particles. Slowly pour lentils into boiling liquid so that it continues to boil. Lower heat to a simmer and cook, covered, for 20 minutes. Check after 10 minutes. If lentils are dry, add a half cup of water. If there is liquid left in the pan after 20 minutes, remove the lid and let boil several minutes until it evaporates. Add olive oil, oregano, and salt and pepper to taste and serve with the meat loaf.

Makes 2 servings

PER SERVING: 256 calories (28 percent from fat), 8.0 g fat (1.1 g saturated, 5.2 g monounsaturated), 0 mg cholesterol, 14.0 g protein, 34.0 g carbohydrates, 6.4 g fiber, 290 mg sodium

SHOPPING LIST

Meat
- 99% fat-free ground white meat turkey (¾ pound needed)

Grocery
- 1 small container fennel seeds
- 1 small container red-pepper flakes
- 1 small container plain bread crumbs
- 1 package chopped or diced frozen onion
- 1 small jar low-fat, low-sodium pasta sauce
- 1 small package dried lentils

Produce
- 1 small package sliced mushrooms

Staples
- Olive oil
- Olive oil spray
- Garlic
- Fat-free, low-sodium chicken broth
- Dried oregano
- Balsamic vinegar
- Egg
- Salt
- Black peppercorns

HELPFUL HINTS

- If pressed for time, use low-fat bottled dressing instead of the recipe given for the spinach.

- Balsamic vinegar can be used instead of sherry wine vinegar.

- Any type of canned beans such as red kidney, navy beans, or black beans can be used.

- A quick way to chop rosemary is to snip the leaves off the stems with a scissors.

COUNTDOWN

- Start chicken.

- While chicken cooks, start beans.

- Make the dressing and add to spinach.

JACQUES PÉPIN'S MEDITERRANEAN CHICKEN OVER SPINACH • GARLIC BEANS

Tender chicken coated with French herbes de Provence and served over a bed of baby spinach salad is a fast dish that master chef and television personality Jacques Pepin told me he likes to make when he's home relaxing with his family.

Herbes de Provence is a mixture of dried herbs that are grown in the south of France. The assortment usually contains marjoram, rosemary, sage, summer savory, thyme, and lavender. It can be found in some supermarkets. If difficult to find, use equal amounts of dried sage and thyme in this recipe.

Dessert Suggestion: Strawberries in Grand Marnier (page 200) goes well with this meal.

Jacques Pépin's Mediterranean Chicken

¾ pound boneless, skinless chicken breast

2 tablespoons herbes de Provence

2 teaspoons olive oil

FOR THE SPINACH SALAD:

2 tablespoons sherry wine vinegar

2 teaspoons Dijon mustard

1 teaspoon olive oil

2 tablespoons water

Salt and freshly ground black pepper

4 cups washed, ready-to-eat baby spinach leaves

Remove fat from chicken and rub with herbes de Provence, making sure to coat both sides. Heat olive oil in a nonstick skillet over medium-high heat. Add chicken and cook 3 minutes. Turn and cook 2 minutes. Remove from heat, cover tightly with a lid, and let sit 10 minutes. A meat thermometer inserted in the thickest portion should read 170 degrees.

TO MAKE THE SPINACH SALAD:

While the chicken rests, whisk vinegar and mustard together in a large salad bowl. Add olive oil and water and whisk until smooth. Add salt and pepper to taste. Add spinach and toss well.

To serve, divide spinach between 2 dinner plates. Slice chicken into strips and arrange them over the spinach. Spoon pan juices over chicken.

Makes 2 servings

PER SERVING: 277 calories (31 percent from fat), 9.5 g fat (1.6 g saturated, 5.6 g monounsaturated), 96 mg cholesterol, 41.6 g protein, 6.1 g carbohydrates, 3.3 g fiber, 215 mg sodium

Garlic Beans

1½ cups canned cannellini
   beans, rinsed and
   drained

1 tablespoon fresh
   rosemary, snipped
   or chopped, or
   1 teaspoon dried

2 medium cloves garlic,
   crushed

1 cup fat-free, low-
   sodium chicken broth

   Salt and freshly ground
   black pepper

Place beans in a saucepan with rosemary, garlic, and chicken broth. Simmer 5 minutes over low heat. Drain the beans and add salt and pepper to taste.

Makes 2 servings

PER SERVING: 244 calories (3 percent from fat), 0.8 g fat (0.3 g saturated, 0.1 g monounsaturated), 0 mg cholesterol, 15.3 g protein, 45.4 g carbohydrates, 10.3 g fiber, 154 mg sodium

SHOPPING LIST

Meat

- Boneless, skinless chicken breast (¾ pound needed)

Grocery

- 1 small container herbes de Provence (or substitute dried sage and thyme)
- 1 bottle sherry wine vinegar
- 1 can cannellini beans

Produce

- 1 bag washed, ready-to-eat baby spinach leaves
- 1 bunch fresh rosemary

Staples

- Olive oil
- Dijon mustard
- Garlic
- Fat-free, low-sodium chicken broth
- Salt
- Black peppercorns

HELPFUL HINT

- Fresh green bell pepper can be used instead of frozen. Add it to the boiling water with the rice instead of at the end of the cooking time.

COUNTDOWN

- Place water for rice on to boil.
- Prepare chicken ingredients.
- Make rice.
- While rice cooks, make chicken.

MEXICAN ORANGE CHICKEN • GREEN PEPPER RICE

Chicken cooked in a savory orange sauce is an unusual, tangy Mexican dish. Rice tossed with green peppers makes a simple side dish.

Dessert Suggestion: Mocha-Cream Cake (page 197) goes well with this meal.

Mexican Orange Chicken

3 tablespoons all-purpose flour

Salt and freshly ground black pepper

2 6-ounce boneless, skinless chicken breasts

1 teaspoon olive oil

½ cup coarsely chopped or diced red onion

2 cloves garlic, crushed

½ cup orange juice

4 orange slices for garnish (optional)

Place flour on a plate and season with salt and pepper to taste. Dip chicken breasts into seasoned flour, making sure all sides are coated. Shake off excess flour. Heat olive oil in a medium-size nonstick skillet over medium-high heat. Add the chicken, onion, and garlic. Brown chicken 2 minutes, turn, and brown second side 2 minutes. Remove chicken to a plate and salt and pepper the cooked sides. Stir the orange juice into the skillet, scraping up the brown bits on the bottom. Lower heat to medium and return chicken to skillet. Cover with a lid and cook, gently, for 5 minutes, until chicken is no longer pink inside. A meat thermometer inserted in the thickest portion should read 170 degrees. Serve with Green Pepper Rice (opposite page) and garnish with orange slices, if using.

Makes 2 servings

PER SERVING: 318 calories (13 percent from fat), 4.7 g fat (0.9 g saturated, 2.2 g monounsaturated), 96 mg cholesterol, 41.9 g protein, 25.5 g carbohydrates, 2.2 g fiber, 110 mg sodium

Green Pepper Rice

1 cup water

¾ cup 10-minute brown rice

1 cup diced or chopped frozen green bell pepper, defrosted

2 teaspoons olive oil

Salt and freshly ground black pepper

Bring water to a boil in a large saucepan over high heat. Stir in rice, return to a boil, reduce heat to medium, cover, and simmer 5 minutes. Remove from heat and stir in the green bell pepper. Cover and let stand 5 minutes. Or, cook rice according to package instructions and add the green pepper at the end. Let sit, covered, 5 minutes. Add oil and salt and pepper to taste. Fluff with a fork.

Makes 2 servings

PER SERVING: 231 calories (23 percent from fat), 6.0 g fat (0.9 g saturated, 3.8 g monounsaturated), 0 mg cholesterol, 4.3 g protein, 40.5 g carbohydrates, 3.0 g fiber, 5 mg sodium

SHOPPING LIST

Meat

- Boneless, skinless chicken breasts (¾ pound needed)

Grocery

- Frozen diced or chopped green bell pepper

Staples

- All-purpose flour
- Garlic
- Red onion
- Olive oil
- Orange juice
- 10-minute brown rice
- Salt
- Black peppercorns

This meal contains 489
calories with 29 percent
of calories from fat.

HELPFUL HINTS

- When using dried
  tarragon, make sure the
  bottle is less than 6
  months old.

- You should extract ⅔ cup
  tomato juice from the
  tomato. If not, use
  another tomato or add a
  little tomato paste and
  water to make up the
  difference.

COUNTDOWN

- Place water on to boil for
  rice.

- Start chicken.

- While chicken cooks,
  make sauce.

POACHED CHICKEN WITH FRESH TOMATO-MAYONNAISE SAUCE • RICE SALAD

Dress up chicken with this fresh tomato-mayonnaise sauce. Poaching the chicken and letting it cool in the liquid keeps the chicken juicy and moist. It can be served hot or cold, and with this cooking method, it keeps well and tastes great the second day.

The addition of juice taken from tomato pulp to the mayonnaise creates a refreshing topping for the poached chicken.

Dessert Suggestion: Spiced Oranges (page 199) go well with this meal.

Poached Chicken with Fresh Tomato-Mayonnaise Sauce

¾ pound boneless,
   skinless chicken breast

1 cup fat-free, low-
   sodium chicken broth

1 medium tomato

¼ cup reduced-fat
   mayonnaise

   Salt and freshly ground
   black pepper

Place chicken in a small saucepan. Add the chicken broth. The chicken should be covered with broth. If not, add water to cover chicken. Bring the broth to a gentle simmer and cook chicken 5 minutes. (Do not allow to boil or chicken will not be as tender as possible.) Remove pan from the heat and let the chicken cool down in the broth for 10 minutes. Cut the tomato in half and scoop out the seeds and pulp into a measuring cup (there should be about ⅔ cup of the juice). Chop the tomato flesh (there should be about 1 cup). Mix the tomato juice with the mayonnaise until smooth. Add salt and pepper to taste. Remove chicken from broth, save ¼ cup broth for the Rice Salad (opposite page), and sprinkle chicken with salt and pepper to taste. Place on 2 dinner plates and spoon mayonnaise sauce over the top. Scatter the chopped tomato over the sauce.

Makes 2 servings

PER SERVING: 287 calories (38 percent from fat), 12.1 g fat (2.1 g saturated, 3.4 g monounsaturated), 106 mg cholesterol, 40.2 g protein, 6.1 g carbohydrates, 1.1 g fiber, 353 mg sodium

Rice Salad

1 cup water

1 cup 10-minute brown rice

1 teaspoon dried tarragon

1 cup cucumber cubes

1 teaspoon olive oil

¼ cup broth from poached chicken

Salt and freshly ground black pepper

Bring water to a boil in a saucepan over high heat. Stir in rice, return to a boil, reduce heat to medium, cover, and simmer 5 minutes. Remove from heat and let stand, covered, 5 minutes. Add tarragon and cucumber and mix well. Add oil, reserved ¼ cup broth from poached chicken, and salt and pepper to taste. Fluff with a fork. Spoon Rice Salad onto plates and serve.

Makes 2 servings

PER SERVING: 202 calories (17 percent from fat), 3.7 g fat (0.6 g saturated, 2.2 g monounsaturated), 0 mg cholesterol, 4.5 g protein, 37.7 g carbohydrates, 2.1 g fiber, 76 mg sodium

SHOPPING LIST

Meat

• Boneless, skinless chicken breast (¾ pound needed)

Grocery

• 1 small container dried tarragon

Produce

• 1 cucumber

• 1 medium tomato

Staples

• 10-minute brown rice

• Olive oil

• Fat-free, low-sodium chicken broth

• Reduced-fat mayonnaise

• Salt

• Black peppercorns

HELPFUL HINTS

- Make sure the package says ground white meat chicken. If it says ground chicken, then skin, fat, and dark meat may be included.

- If pressed for time, buy coleslaw from the deli.

- Sugar or sugar substitute can be used in the coleslaw recipe.

COUNTDOWN

- Make slaw.
- Prepare chicken burgers.

SOUTHWESTERN CHICKEN BURGERS • QUICK SLAW

Spicy tomato salsa gives these light, juicy burgers a hint of the Southwest. Making fresh coleslaw that is tangy and crunchy is a breeze using shredded cabbage or coleslaw mix available in the produce department of the supermarket.

Coleslaw tastes even better the second day. Double the recipe and you will have a ready-made salad for another day.

Dessert Suggestion: Lemon-Lime Pineapple Slices (page 195) goes well with this meal.

Southwestern Chicken Burgers

¾ **pound ground white meat chicken**

¼ **cup no-sugar-added tomato salsa**

Salt and freshly ground black pepper

Olive oil spray

2 **whole wheat or whole grain hamburger rolls**

1 **medium tomato, sliced**

2 **lettuce leaves**

Mix chicken, salsa, and salt and black pepper to taste together in a small bowl. Shape into burgers about 4 inches round and ¼ to ½ inch thick. Heat a nonstick skillet over medium-high heat. Coat with olive oil spray and cook burgers 5 minutes on each side. A meat thermometer inserted into the thickest portion should read 170 degrees. Meanwhile, coat hamburger rolls with olive oil spray and toast in a toaster oven. Place cooked chicken burgers on bottom half of each roll. Place 1 tomato slice on top. Garnish the plate with extra slices of tomato. Cover the tomato with lettuce leaf. Close with top of roll and serve.

Makes 2 servings

PER SERVING: 332 calories (15 percent from fat), 5.7 g fat (1.2 g saturated, 1.3 g monounsaturated), 96 mg cholesterol, 45.0 g protein, 25.6 g carbohydrates, 5.0 g fiber, 477 mg sodium

Quick Slaw

2 tablespoons mayonnaise

2 tablespoons distilled white vinegar

Sugar substitute equivalent to 1 teaspoon sugar

Salt and freshly ground black pepper

4 slices red onion (½ cup)

1 cup washed, ready-to-eat shredded carrots

2 cups washed, ready-to-eat shredded cabbage

Mix mayonnaise, vinegar, and sugar substitute together in a medium-size bowl. Add salt and pepper to taste. Add onion, carrots, and cabbage. Toss well. Add more salt and pepper, if needed. Set aside while chicken burgers cook.

Makes 2 servings

PER SERVING: 164 calories (80 percent from fat), 14.5 g fat (2.0 g saturated, 4.8 g monounsaturated), 10 mg cholesterol, 8.1 g protein, 33.7 g carbohydrates, 5.4 g fiber, 112 mg sodium

SHOPPING LIST

Meat

- Cround white meat chicken (¾ pound needed)

Grocery

- 1 small jar tomato salsa
- 1 small package whole wheat or whole grain hamburger rolls

Produce

- 1 medium tomato
- 1 bag washed, ready-to-eat shredded cabbage
- 1 bag washed, ready-to-eat shredded carrots
- 1 small head lettuce

Staples

- Mayonnaise
- White vinegar
- Olive oil spray
- Red onion
- Sugar substitute
- Salt
- Black peppercorns

TURKEY SKILLET CASSEROLE • TOSSED SALAD

This one-pot meal is a hearty stove-top casserole with a light touch. The noodles cook right in the sauce, so it's easy to serve it right from the stove. Look for 99% fat-free ground turkey that is made from breast or white meat only. If the package simply says "ground turkey," it may contain skin and fat.

Dessert Suggestion: Plum Meringue (page 198) goes well with this meal.

Turkey Skillet Casserole

2 teaspoons olive oil

1 cup chopped onion

2 medium cloves garlic, crushed

¾ pound 99% fat-free ground turkey breast

1½ cups low-fat, low-sodium pasta sauce

1 cup water

1 cup sliced portobello mushrooms

2 ounces whole wheat noodles (about 1 cup)

Salt and freshly ground black pepper

¼ cup reduced-fat, shredded sharp Cheddar cheese

2 tablespoons reduced-fat sour cream

Heat oil in a nonstick skillet over medium-high heat. Add onion and garlic. Cook 3 minutes. Add the turkey, breaking it up with the edge of a cooking spoon. Add the pasta sauce, water, mushrooms, and noodles. Add salt and pepper to taste. Stir to mix well. Reduce heat to medium-low, cover with a lid, and simmer, stirring once or twice, until noodles are cooked, about 15 minutes. Stir in the Cheddar cheese and top with a spoonful of sour cream.

Makes 2 servings

PER SERVING: 506 calories (16 percent from fat), 9.0 g fat (2.8 g saturated, 4.4 g monounsaturated), 117 mg cholesterol, 56.4 g protein, 52.3 g carbohydrates, 6.1 g fiber, 738 mg sodium

Tossed Salad

4 cups washed, ready-to-eat green salad

2 tablespoons reduced-fat oil and vinegar dressing

Place salad in a bowl and toss with dressing.

Makes 2 servings

PER SERVING: 42 calories (53 percent from fat), 2.5 g fat (0.2 g saturated, 0 g monounsaturated), 0 mg cholesterol, 2.0 g protein, 3.9 g carbohydrates, 2.2 g fiber, 122 mg sodium

HELPFUL HINTS

- Prepared horseradish can be used instead of wasabi powder.

- Any low-fat oil and vinegar dressing can be used.

COUNTDOWN

- Make chicken and sauce.
- Make Pan-Roasted Corn and Broccoli.

WASABI CHICKEN • PAN-ROASTED CORN AND BROCCOLI

Spicy wasabi sauce gives pan-seared chicken an Asian flavor. Corn and ginger tossed with broccoli complete this Pacific Rim dinner.

Wasabi is the Japanese version of horseradish. It's an Asian root vegetable that is sold in paste and powdered form. The powdered form is mixed with water to form a thick paste. The powder loses its flavor quickly, so make sure it's fresh. The green wasabi served with sushi is usually white wasabi powder that has been mixed with coloring and mustard. Fresh wasabi root can be found in some Asian stores.

To save washing an extra pan, use the same skillet for the chicken and the vegetables.

Dessert Suggestion: Strawberries in Grand Marnier (page 200) goes well with this meal.

Wasabi Chicken

2 tablespoons reduced-fat oil and vinegar dressing

2 teaspoons wasabi powder

¾ pound boneless, skinless chicken breast

1 teaspoon canola oil

Salt and freshly ground black pepper

Mix the dressing with the wasabi powder and set aside. Flatten chicken with the smooth side of a meat mallet, the bottom of a heavy skillet, or your palm to ¼ inch thick. Heat oil in a large nonstick skillet over medium-high heat. Add the chicken and sear 4 minutes. Turn and sear the other side for 4 minutes, until chicken is no longer pink inside and juices run clear. Sprinkle salt and pepper to taste on the cooked sides. Remove skillet from heat and place chicken on a plate. Drizzle the reserved wasabi sauce over the chicken. Cover with another plate or foil to keep warm until the vegetables are ready. Use the same skillet for the side dish (recipe on opposite page).

Makes 2 servings

PER SERVING: 235 calories (25 percent from fat), 6.6 g fat (1.1 g saturated, 2.2 g monounsaturated), 96 mg cholesterol, 39.5 g protein, 1.9 g carbohydrates, 0.4 g fiber, 222 mg sodium

Pan-Roasted Corn and Broccoli

2 teaspoons canola oil

2 teaspoons ground ginger

3 cups frozen corn kernels

½ pound broccoli florets (about 3 cups)

1 medium red bell pepper, sliced (about 1 cup)

Salt and freshly ground black pepper

Add the oil to the nonstick skillet used for the chicken and heat over medium-high heat. Add the ginger, corn, broccoli, and bell pepper. Toss to coat the vegetables with the oil and cover with a lid. Cook 5 minutes, turn vegetables over, and cook, covered, 5 more minutes. Add salt and pepper to taste.

Makes 2 servings

PER SERVING: 295 calories (19 percent from fat), 6.2 g fat (0.9 g saturated, 3.7 g monounsaturated), 0 mg cholesterol, 11.4 g protein, 60.1 g carbohydrates, 11.3 g fiber, 50 mg sodium

SHOPPING LIST

Meat

- Boneless, skinless chicken breast (¾ pound needed)

Grocery

- 1 small container ground ginger
- 1 small package frozen corn kernels
- 1 small container wasabi powder

Produce

- ½ pound broccoli florets
- 1 medium red bell pepper

Staples

- Canola oil
- Reduced-fat oil and vinegar dressing
- Salt
- Black peppercorns

PORK, BEEF, LAMB, VEAL, AND MEATLESS

Photo on page 59.

HELPFUL HINTS

- A quick way to chop ginger is to grate it with the skin on.

- For easy stir-frying, place all of the prepared ingredients on a cutting board or plate in order of use. You won't have to look at the recipe once you start to cook.

- Make sure the wok or skillet is very hot before adding the ingredients.

COUNTDOWN

- Make rice.
- While rice cooks, prepare ingredients.
- Stir-fry pork.

CHINESE PORK IN LETTUCE PUFFS •
BROWN RICE AND PEAS

While at a Chinese celebration, I tasted savory pork wrapped in lettuce puffs with slivers of cool cucumber and tangy scallions. In addition to being delicious, it had a crisp texture and made a unique presentation.

A small amount of dry sherry is called for in the pork recipe. You can buy small bottles or splits of sherry at most liquor stores.

Hoisin sauce can be found in the Chinese section of the supermarket. It is a paste made from soybeans, vinegar, sugar, and spices.

As with most Asian dishes, it takes a few minutes to assemble the ingredients, but then it takes only about 5 minutes to cook.

Chinese Pork in Lettuce Puffs

1 tablespoon low-sodium soy sauce

1 tablespoon dry sherry

2 medium cloves garlic, crushed

1 tablespoon chopped fresh ginger

1 tablespoon honey

¾ pound pork tenderloin, visible fat removed, cut into ½-inch pieces

2 teaspoons sesame oil
 Salt and freshly ground black pepper

Mix soy sauce, sherry, garlic, ginger, and honey together in a bowl. Add pork to marinade while you prepare the garnishes.

TO PREPARE GARNISHES

Wash and remove root end and damaged leaves from scallions. Cut into 4-inch pieces. Slice each piece lengthwise into long slivers. Place in small bowl. Peel and cut cucumber into 4-inch pieces, then cut lengthwise into thin slivers. Place in another small bowl. Remove lettuce leaves from lettuce in whole pieces. They will form a cup. Wash and drain them. Place in large serving bowl. Spoon hoisin sauce into small serving bowl.

FOR GARNISH:

- 2 scallions (about ½ cup)
- ½ medium cucumber
- 4 large iceberg lettuce leaves
- 3 tablespoons hoisin sauce

TO MAKE PORK

Heat sesame oil in a wok or skillet on high heat until smoking. Add pork and marinade mixture to the wok. Separate any pieces that cling together. Cook without stirring for 1 minute. Turn and stir-fry 2 minutes. Sprinkle with salt and pepper to taste. Spoon into a small bowl.

To serve, place bowls with scallions, cucumber, lettuce, hoisin sauce, and pork on the table. Take 1 lettuce leaf and spoon a little sauce onto it. Add a few scallions, cucumber slivers, and some pork. Roll up and eat like a sandwich.

Makes 2 servings

PER SERVING: 380 calories (27 percent from fat), 11.5 g fat (2.8 g saturated, 6.2 g monounsaturated), 108 mg cholesterol, 39.8 g protein, 28.0 g carbohydrates, 3.7 g fiber, 751 mg sodium

Brown Rice and Peas

- 1 cup water
- 1 cup 10-minute brown rice
- 1 cup frozen petite peas
- 3 teaspoons sesame oil
  Salt and freshly ground black pepper

Bring the water to a boil in a medium-size saucepan over high heat. Add rice, cover, and simmer 5 minutes. Remove from heat, add peas, replace the cover, and let sit 5 minutes. Add sesame oil and salt and pepper to taste. Toss well.

Makes 2 servings

PER SERVING: 267 calories (21 percent from fat), 6.1 g fat (0.9 g saturated, 3.8 g monounsaturated), 0 mg cholesterol, 7.4 g protein, 45.6 g carbohydrates, 4.6 g fiber, 84 mg sodium

SHOPPING LIST

Meat

- Pork tenderloin (¾ pound needed)

Grocery

- 1 small bottle dry sherry
- 1 small bottle low-sodium soy sauce
- 1 small bottle hoisin sauce
- 1 small package frozen petite peas
- 1 bottle sesame oil

Produce

- 1 small bunch scallions
- 1 medium cucumber
- 1 small head iceberg lettuce
- 1 small piece fresh ginger

Staples

- Garlic
- Honey
- 10-minute brown rice
- Salt
- Black peppercorns

Photo on page 60.

HELPFUL HINTS

- Frozen diced onion and green pepper can be substituted for fresh to save time.

- White cannellini beans can be used instead of red beans. They will give a softer, lighter texture to the dish.

- Serve this chili with bowls of sour cream, chopped onion, and chopped fresh cilantro as garnishes, along with some rice.

- Chili freezes well. If you have time, double the recipe and freeze half for another quick dinner.

COUNTDOWN

- Prepare ingredients.
- Make chili.

MEXICAN PORK AND BEAN CHILI • SHREDDED LETTUCE SALAD

This incredible chili takes only 20 minutes to make. The degree of heat is up to you. Add more chili powder or fresh chile peppers as you like.

Mexican Pork and Bean Chili

2 teaspoons olive oil

½ medium onion, sliced (1 cup), divided use

½ pound pork tenderloin, fat removed and cut into ½-inch cubes

1 celery stalk, sliced (½ cup)

1 small green pepper, sliced (1½ cups)

2 cups canned red kidney beans, rinsed and drained

2 cups canned no-salt-added chopped tomatoes

½ cup frozen or canned and drained corn kernels

1½ tablespoons chili powder

2 teaspoons ground cumin seed

Salt and freshly ground black pepper

FOR GARNISH:

½ cup reduced-fat sour cream

½ cup chopped fresh cilantro

Heat oil in a large nonstick skillet over high heat. Set aside 2 tablespoons of the sliced onion for garnish. Add the meat, celery, green pepper, and remaining onion to the skillet. Cook 5 minutes, tossing to brown meat on all sides. Add beans, tomatoes, corn, chili powder, and cumin seed. Lower heat to medium and simmer 15 minutes. Add salt and pepper to taste. Serve chili in large bowls. Place the sour cream, cilantro, and reserved onion into small bowls and pass with the chili.

Makes 2 servings

PER SERVING: 598 calories (23 percent from fat), 15.1 g fat (4.7 g saturated, 6.9 g monounsaturated), 84 mg cholesterol, 44.3 g protein, 76.6 g carbohydrates, 29.4 g fiber, 727 mg sodium

Shredded Lettuce Salad

4 cups washed, ready-to-eat mixed salad

2 tablespoons reduced-fat olive oil and vinegar dressing

Place salad in a bowl and toss with dressing.

Makes 2 servings

PER SERVING: 42 calories (53 percent from fat), 2.5 g fat (0.2 g saturated, 0 g monounsaturated), 0 mg cholesterol, 2.0 g protein, 3.9 g carbohydrates, 2.2 g fiber, 122 mg sodium

SHOPPING LIST

Dairy
- 1 small container reduced-fat sour cream

Meat
- Pork tenderloin (8 ounces needed)

Grocery
- 1 can red kidney beans
- 1 can no-salt-added chopped tomatoes
- 1 small container chili powder
- 1 small container ground cumin seed
- 1 package frozen or 1 can corn kernels

Produce
- 1 small bunch celery
- 1 small green pepper
- 1 small bunch cilantro
- 1 bag washed, ready-to-eat mixed salad

Staples
- Olive oil
- Onion
- Reduced-fat olive oil and vinegar dressing
- Salt
- Black peppercorns

Photo on back cover.

HELPFUL HINTS

- Any type of quick-cooking steak can be substituted for sirloin: flank, skirt, or strip.

- Yellow or red potatoes can be substituted for baby yellow potatoes; cut the bigger potatoes into 1-inch pieces.

- Use the same skillet to cook the mushrooms, then the steak, and to finish the potatoes.

COUNTDOWN

- Cook mushrooms.
- Start the potatoes.
- Make mushroom pesto sauce.
- Cook the steak.
- Finish the potatoes.

MUSHROOM PESTO STEAK • HOT PEPPER POTATOES

It seems everyone loves a juicy steak, and it can certainly be part of a balanced, healthful meal. A mushroom pesto sauce goes perfectly with a pan-roasted steak. Meaty portobello mushrooms make the base for this pesto sauce. Pesto sauce made with fresh basil, parsley, olive oil, and Parmesan cheese originated in Genoa, Italy. Adding mushrooms gives an earthy flavor to the sauce. This dinner is perfect for a weekend or simple enough for a weekday as well.

Open a bag of washed, ready-to-eat lettuce to complete this meal.

Mushroom Pesto Steak

Olive oil spray

¼ pound sliced portobello mushrooms (about 1⅔ cups)

¼ cup water

2 tablespoons prepared pesto sauce

¾ pound sirloin steak, visible fat removed

Salt and freshly ground black pepper

Several sprigs watercress

Heat a nonstick skillet over medium-high heat. Coat with olive oil spray. Add mushrooms and cook 1 minute, turn, and cook 1 minute longer. Transfer to a food processor and add the water and pesto sauce. Blend until smooth. Set aside. Add the steak to the same skillet. Sear over high heat for 1 minute, turn, and sear 1 minute. Turn heat down to medium and cook 5 minutes for rare. A meat thermometer inserted in the thickest portion should read 145 degrees. For medium doneness, cook another 2 minutes (160 degrees). Sprinkle the steak with salt and pepper to taste and spoon the reserved sauce on top. Use the same skillet for the Hot Pepper Potatoes (opposite page). Place watercress on the plate for a garnish.

Makes 2 servings

PER SERVING: 351 calories (47 percent from fat), 18.2 g fat (4.9 g saturated, 8.2 g monounsaturated), 107 mg cholesterol, 39.6 g protein, 4.6 g carbohydrates, 1.2 g fiber, 245 mg sodium

Hot Pepper Potatoes

1 pound baby yellow
potatoes

2 teaspoons olive oil

Several drops hot-
pepper sauce

Salt and freshly ground
black pepper

Wash potatoes. Slice in half (do not peel). Place in a large saucepan and fill with cold water to cover the potatoes. Bring to a boil over high heat, cover, and cook 10 minutes, or until potatoes are cooked through. Drain. When steak is removed from the skillet, add the olive oil and hot-pepper sauce to the skillet. Heat over high heat. Add the potatoes and toss until crisp and golden, about 3 minutes. Add salt and pepper to taste. Serve with the steak.

Makes 2 servings

PER SERVING: 220 calories (19 percent from fat), 4.7 g fat (0.7 g saturated, 3.3 g monounsaturated), 0 mg cholesterol, 4.9 g protein, 41.0 g carbohydrates, 3.0 g fiber, 13 mg sodium

SHOPPING LIST

Meat

- Sirloin steak
  (¾ pound needed)

Grocery

- 1 small container pesto
  sauce

Produce

- 1 small container sliced
  portobello mushrooms
- 1 small bunch watercress
- 1 pound baby yellow
  potatoes

Staples

- Olive oil spray
- Olive oil
- Hot-pepper sauce
- Salt
- Black peppercorns

PORTOBELLO PARMESAN OVER LINGUINE

In this hearty vegetarian dish, a takeoff of traditional eggplant parmesan, meaty portobello mushrooms are dressed in a rich tomato sauce and covered with mozzarella cheese. For this quick meal, the ingredients are placed in a skillet and cooked in 8 minutes.

Portobello Parmesan

2 teaspoons olive oil

1 pound sliced portobello mushrooms

1 teaspoon dried oregano

Salt and freshly ground black pepper

2 cups low-fat, low-sodium tomato sauce

1 cup fresh basil, torn into large pieces

½ cup shredded, part-skim milk mozzarella cheese

½ cup grated Parmesan cheese

Heat oil in a large nonstick skillet over medium-high heat. Add the mushrooms and sprinkle with the oregano and salt and pepper to taste. Cook for 3 minutes. Add the tomato sauce and basil and mix well. Place shredded mozzarella over the sauce and cover the skillet. Simmer 5 minutes to warm the sauce and melt the cheese. Sprinkle Parmesan cheese on top.

Makes 2 servings

PER SERVING: 329 calories (44 percent from fat), 15.9 g fat (7.4 g saturated, 6.4 g monounsaturated), 32 mg cholesterol, 26.3 g protein, 23.9 g carbohydrates, 6.1 g fiber, 557 mg sodium

Linguine

¼ pound whole wheat linguine

1 teaspoon olive oil

Salt and freshly ground black pepper

Place a large sauce pan with 3 to 4 quarts of water on to boil over high heat. Add linguine in boiling water for 3 minutes if using fresh or 9 minutes if using dry linguine. Drain and toss with olive oil and add salt and pepper to taste. Place linguine on dinner plates and top with Portobello Parmesan.

Makes 2 servings

PER SERVING: 218 calories (13 percent from fat), 3.1 g fat (0.5 g saturated, 1.8 g monounsaturated), 0 mg cholesterol, 8.3 g protein, 42.8 g carbohydrates, 0 g fiber, 5 mg sodium

SHOPPING LIST

Dairy

- 1 package shredded, part-skim milk mozzarella cheese
- 1 package Parmesan cheese

Grocery

- 1 can low-fat, low-sodium tomato sauce
- 1 package whole wheat linguine

Produce

- 1 pound sliced porto-bello mushrooms
- 1 bunch basil

Staples

- Olive oil
- Dried oregano
- Salt
- Black peppercorns

ROSEMARY-GARLIC LAMB STEAK • ITALIAN TOMATOES AND BEANS

A steak cut from the leg of lamb is tender and juicy and cooks in minutes. Crushed garlic and rosemary is all that's needed to enhance the natural flavor. The Italian Tomatoes and Beans can be cooked on the stove top or in a microwave oven. Both directions are given.

Dessert Suggestion: Honey-Cinnamon Apples (page 194) goes well with this meal.

Rosemary-Garlic Lamb Steak

2 6-ounce lamb steaks center cut from leg

2 medium cloves garlic, crushed

1 tablespoon fresh rosemary, chopped, or 1 teaspoon crushed or dried

Salt and freshly ground black pepper

Olive oil spray

Remove visible fat from lamb. Sprinkle with garlic, rosemary, and salt and pepper to taste. Press the garlic and rosemary into the lamb on both sides. Heat a nonstick skillet over medium-high heat and coat with olive oil spray. Cook lamb 2 minutes. Coat the lamb with olive oil spray and turn. Cook 2 minutes for a ¾-inch-thick steak. A meat thermometer inserted in the thickest portion should read 125 degrees for rare. Leave the lamb steak 1 to 2 minutes longer for medium rare. A meat thermometer should read 145 degrees. If using 1 large steak weighing 12 ounces, cut in half before serving.

Makes 2 servings

PER SERVING: 264 calories (42 percent from fat), 12.3 g fat (3.7 g saturated, 3.7 g monounsaturated), 108 mg cholesterol, 34.6 g protein, 2.1 g carbohydrates, 0.8 g fiber, 109 mg sodium

Italian Tomatoes and Beans

1 cup sliced red onion

1 cup no-salt-added diced tomatoes

2 medium cloves garlic, crushed

1½ cups rinsed and drained cannellini beans

Salt and freshly ground black pepper

Stove-top method: Cook onion, tomatoes, and garlic for 3 minutes in a large saucepan over medium-high heat. Add beans and cook 3 minutes longer. Add salt and pepper to taste.

Microwave method: Place onion, tomatoes, and garlic in a large microwaveable bowl and cover with a paper towel or plate. Microwave on high 3 minutes. Remove, stir, and add the beans. Microwave on high 2 minutes. Add salt and pepper to taste and mix well.

Makes 2 servings

PER SERVING: 291 calories (2 percent from fat), 0.8 g fat (0.2 g saturated, 0.1 g monounsaturated), 0 mg cholesterol, 16.3 g protein, 57.4 g carbohydrates, 11.9 g fiber, 25 mg sodium

SHOPPING LIST

Meat

- Lamb steaks center cut from the leg (¾ pound needed)

Grocery

- 1 can cannellini beans
- 1 small can no-salt-added diced tomatoes

Produce

- 1 small bunch fresh rosemary (or 1 small bottle crushed or dried rosemary)

Staples

- Garlic
- Olive oil spray
- Red onion
- Salt
- Black peppercorns

HELPFUL HINTS

- Low-sodium soy sauce can be substituted for the hoisin sauce.

- Angel-hair pasta can be substituted for Chinese noodles.

- A quick way to slice scallions is to snip them with a scissors.

- A quick way to chop ginger is to grate it with the skin on.

- For easy cooking, place the prepared ingredients on a cutting board or plate in order of use. You won't have to look at the recipe once you start to cook.

- Make sure your wok is very hot before adding the ingredients.

COUNTDOWN

- Place water onto boil for noodles.

- Marinate pork.

- While pork marinates, prepare the other ingredients.

- Cook pork and boil noodles.

STIR-FRIED DICED PORK • CHINESE NOODLES

Garlic, sherry, hoisin sauce, and almonds flavor diced pork in this quick Chinese stir-fry.

As with most Asian-style recipes, it takes a few minutes to assemble the ingredients, but the cooking time is very short. In this recipe, the pork is ready in only 5 minutes. The secret to this quick-cooked dish is cutting the pork into ½-inch pieces.

Hoisin sauce is a mixture of soybeans, garlic, chile peppers, and spices. It can be found in the Asian section of the supermarket.

A small amount of dry sherry is called for in the pork recipe. You can buy small bottles or splits of sherry at most liquor stores.

Dessert Suggestion: Honey-Cinnamon Apples (page 194) goes well with this meal.

Stir-Fried Diced Pork

¼ cup dry sherry

4 medium cloves garlic, crushed

1 tablespoon chopped fresh ginger or 1 teaspoon ground

¾ pound pork tenderloin, visible fat removed and cut into ½-inch cubes

2 tablespoons cornstarch

1 tablespoon hoisin sauce

1 tablespoon water

2 teaspoons canola oil

1 cup sliced celery

2 tablespoons slivered almonds

Salt and freshly ground black pepper

2 scallions, sliced (about ½ cup)

Mix sherry, garlic, and ginger together. Marinate the pork in sherry mixture for 5 minutes while preparing other ingredients. Remove pork from mixture to a plate, reserving marinade. Sprinkle cornstarch over pork, toss together, and set aside. Mix hoisin sauce and water with reserved marinade. Heat oil in a wok or skillet and add pork to the wok. Stir-fry 1 minute. Add celery and almonds and stir-fry 1 minute. Add marinade to the wok and toss 30 seconds. Add salt and pepper to taste. Scatter scallions on top and spoon over Chinese Noodles (opposite page).

Makes 2 servings

PER SERVING: 413 calories (34 percent from fat), 15.7 g fat (3.2 g saturated, 6.7 g monounsaturated), 108 mg cholesterol, 38.5 g protein, 21.8 g carbohydrates, 2.7 g fiber, 273 mg sodium

Chinese Noodles

4 ounces steamed or
 fresh Chinese noodles

2 teaspoons canola oil

 Salt and freshly ground
 black pepper

Bring a large saucepan filled with water to a boil. Add the noodles and cook 1 to 2 minutes. Drain and toss with oil. Add salt and pepper to taste. Serve pork over noodles.

Makes 2 servings

PER SERVING: 256 calories (24 percent from fat), 6.9 g fat (0.7 g saturated, 4.1 g monounsaturated), 54 mg cholesterol, 8.0 g protein, 40.4 g carbohydrates, 1.5 g fiber, 12 mg sodium

SHOPPING LIST

Meat

- Pork tenderloin
  (¾ pound needed)

Grocery

- 1 small bottle dry sherry
- 1 small bottle hoisin sauce
- 1 small package slivered almonds
- 1 small package Chinese noodles

Produce

- 1 small piece fresh ginger (or ground ginger)
- 1 small bunch celery
- 1 small bunch scallions

Staples

- Garlic
- Cornstarch
- Canola oil
- Salt
- Black peppercorns

HELPFUL HINTS

- Any type of blue-veined cheese can be used. Look for crumbled blue-veined cheese in the dairy section of the supermarket.

- Washed and trimmed green beans are available in most supermarkets. Any type of green beans can be used.

- Use a nonstick skillet that just fits the veal in one layer. If the skillet is too small, cook the veal in batches so that the pieces are only in one layer.

COUNTDOWN

- Place water for linguine on to boil.
- Prepare all ingredients.
- Make linguine.
- Make veal.

VEAL ROQUEFORT • LINGUINE AND FRENCH GREEN BEANS

Juicy veal cutlets dressed with the distinct flavor of Roquefort sauce creates a tasty dish from a perfect blend of ingredients. Veal cutlets only take 2 or 3 minutes to cook. They will continue to cook in their own heat once removed from the skillet.

Veal Roquefort

3 tablespoons all-purpose flour
  Salt and freshly ground black pepper
2 6-ounce veal cutlets
  Olive oil spray
½ cup skim milk
1 ounce crumbled Roquefort cheese (about 2½ tablespoons)

Place flour on a plate and season with salt and pepper to taste. Dip the veal cutlets in the flour, making sure both sides are coated. Shake off any extra flour.

Heat a nonstick skillet over medium-high heat and coat with olive oil spray. Add the veal in one layer. Brown 2 minutes and turn over. Brown the second side 1 minute. Transfer to a serving dish and sprinkle with pepper to taste. Add the milk to the skillet and scrape up the brown bits in the bottom of the pan, about 20 seconds. Immediately add the Roquefort cheese and stir to melt the cheese and make a smooth sauce. Taste for seasoning. Add pepper if needed. (The cheese should provide enough salt.) Spoon sauce over cutlets. To serve, place veal and sauce over the Linguine and French Green Beans (opposite page).

Makes 2 servings

PER SERVING: 341 calories (34 percent from fat), 12.8 g fat (5.3 g saturated, 3.1 g monounsaturated), 146 mg cholesterol, 42.0 g protein, 12.2 g carbohydrates, 0.3 g fiber, 397 mg sodium

Linguine and French Green Beans

¼ pound whole wheat
   linguine

¼ pound green beans,
   washed, trimmed, and
   cut in half (about 1 cup)

2 teaspoons olive oil

   Salt and freshly ground
   black pepper

Place a large saucepan with 3 to 4 quarts water on to boil over high heat. Add linguine and beans. Boil 3 minutes if using fresh linguine. If using dried linguine, boil 6 minutes, add beans, and boil 3 minutes longer. Drain, leaving about 2 tablespoons water on the pasta. Add oil and salt and pepper to taste. Toss well.

Makes 2 servings

PER SERVING: 255 calories (19 percent from fat), 5.4 g fat (0.8 g saturated, 3.4 g monounsaturated), 0 mg cholesterol, 9.3 g protein, 46.7 g carbohydrates, 1.9 g fiber, 9 mg sodium

SHOPPING LIST

Dairy

- 1 small package crumbled Roquefort cheese

Meat

- Veal cutlets (¾ pound needed)

Grocery

- 1 package whole wheat linguine

Produce

- ¼ pound green beans

Staples

- All-purpose flour
- Skim milk
- Olive oil spray
- Olive oil
- Salt
- Black peppercorns

This meal contains 590 calories with 30 percent of calories from fat.

Photo on page 61.

HELPFUL HINTS

- Strip, tenderloin, flank, or skirt steak can be used instead of sirloin.
- Thinly slice the fennel with a mandolin or food processor fitted with a slicing blade.

COUNTDOWN

- Make salad and set aside.
- Make steak.

WALNUT-CRUSTED STEAK • FENNEL BEAN SALAD

A juicy steak with a walnut topping and served with Fennel Bean Salad can be a weeknight meal or a special weekend dinner with friends. The nut coating provides a crunchy texture that contrasts with the tender meat. This contrast is echoed by the crunchy fennel and tender bean salad. Aromatic fennel is a great vegetable to use either cooked or raw.

Walnut-Crusted Steak

Olive oil spray

¾ pound sirloin steak, fat removed (about ¾ inches thick)

2 tablespoons hot-pepper jam or jelly

2 tablespoons finely chopped walnuts

Salt and freshly ground black pepper

Heat a nonstick skillet over medium-high heat and coat with olive oil spray. Add steak and cook 5 minutes. Turn and spread the jam over the cooked side. Press the walnuts into the steak. Continue to cook the steak for 5 minutes, for rare. A meat thermometer inserted in the thickest portion should read 145 degrees. Cook 2 minutes longer for medium rare (160 degrees). Sprinkle with salt and pepper to taste.

Makes 2 servings

PER SERVING: 360 calories (41 percent from fat), 16.4 g fat (3.9 g saturated, 4.1 g monounsaturated), 102 mg cholesterol, 37.3 g protein, 13.7 g carbohydrates, 0.5 g fiber, 99 mg sodium

Fennel Bean Salad

1 large fennel bulb, thinly sliced (about 3 cups)

1½ cups red kidney beans, drained and rinsed

2 tablespoons reduced-fat Italian salad dressing

Salt and freshly ground black pepper

Cut the top stem and feathery leaves off the fennel. Reserve the fennel leaves. Wash and slice the fennel bulb. Place sliced fennel and beans in a bowl and add dressing and salt and pepper to taste. Toss well. Snip about 1 tablespoon of the feathery leaves and sprinkle over salad.

Makes 2 servings

PER SERVING: 230 calories (12 percent from fat), 3.1 g fat (0.3 g saturated, 0.1 g monounsaturated), 0 mg cholesterol, 11.9 g protein, 40.7 g carbohydrates, 16.6 g fiber, 189 mg sodium

SHOPPING LIST

Meat

● Sirloin steak (¾ pound needed)

Grocery

● 1 small jar hot-pepper jam or jelly

● 1 small package walnut pieces

● 1 small bottle reduced-fat Italian salad dressing

● 1 can red kidney beans

Produce

● 1 large fennel bulb

Staples

● Olive oil spray

● Salt

● Black peppercorns

DESSERTS

- Use good quality balsamic vinegar.

SHOPPING LIST

Dairy

- 1 small carton whipping cream

Produce

- 1 container strawberries

Staples

- Sugar

- Balsamic vinegar

CREAMY BALSAMIC STRAWBERRIES

A small amount of balsamic vinegar gives an intriguing flavor to strawberries and cream.

2 cups sliced, ripe strawberries

2 teaspoons sugar

1 tablespoon balsamic vinegar

2 tablespoons whipping cream

Divide strawberries between 2 dessert bowls or ramekins. Mix sugar and balsamic vinegar together and drizzle over strawberries. Spoon whipping cream on top.

Makes 2 servings

PER SERVING: 114 calories (48 percent from fat), 6.1 g fat (3.5 g saturated, 1.7 g monounsaturated), 20 mg cholesterol, 1.2 g protein, 15.7 g carbohydrates, 3.5 g fiber, 8 mg sodium

FRUIT COMPOTE

Apples, pears, and raisins are poached in apple juice, flavored with cinnamon and vanilla, for this simple dessert.

1 medium Red Delicious apple

1 pear

2 tablespoons golden raisins

½ cup unsweetened apple juice

1 cinnamon stick

1 teaspoon vanilla extract

Wash, quarter, and core apple and pear. Cut into ¾-inch pieces. Place fruit in saucepan. Add raisins, apple juice, and cinnamon stick. Bring to a boil over high heat, lower heat to medium high, cover, and simmer for 5 minutes, stirring once. Remove fruit with a slotted spoon to 2 dessert bowls. Raise heat and reduce liquid for 3 to 4 minutes. Remove cinnamon stick and discard. Stir in vanilla and spoon over fruit. Cool slightly before serving. It can also be served cold.

Makes 2 servings

PER SERVING: 152 calories (4 percent from fat), 0.7 g fat (0.1 g saturated, 0 g monounsaturated), 0 mg cholesterol, 0.8 g protein, 37.6 g carbohydrates, 4.6 g fiber, 5 mg sodium

HELPFUL HINTS

- The pear doesn't need to be fully ripened.
- Any dried fruit such as dates, prunes, or figs may be substituted for the raisins.

SHOPPING LIST

Grocery

- 1 small bottle unsweetened apple juice
- 1 small package golden raisins
- 1 bottle cinnamon sticks

Produce

- 1 medium Red Delicious apple
- 1 pear

Staples

- Vanilla extract

SHOPPING LIST

Produce

- 2 medium Red Delicious apples
- 1 small container raisins

Staples

- Ground cinnamon
- Honey

HONEY-CINNAMON APPLES

This apple dessert can be ready in 5 minutes with the help of a microwave oven.

2 medium Red Delicious apples, cored and cut into 1-inch pieces (about 2½ cups)

2 tablespoons raisins

1 teaspoon ground cinnamon

1 tablespoon honey

Place apples and raisins in a microwaveable bowl. Sprinkle cinnamon and honey over fruit. Toss well. Microwave on high 3 minutes. Spoon into 2 dessert dishes. Cool slightly before serving.

Makes 2 servings

PER SERVING: 143 calories (4 percent from fat), 0.6 g fat (0.1 g saturated, 0 g monounsaturated), 0 mg cholesterol, 0.6 g protein, 37.6 g carbohydrates, 5.0 g fiber, 4 mg sodium

LEMON-LIME PINEAPPLE SLICES

Assemble this sweet dessert in a few minutes by using fresh pineapple slices, lemon-lime yogurt, and broken pecans. Fresh pineapple slices are available in the produce section of the supermarket.

2 slices pineapple (about 1 cup)

¾ cup fat-free, low-sugar lemon-lime yogurt

1 tablespoon pecan pieces

Place a slice of pineapple on 2 dessert plates. Top each slice with ⅓ cup yogurt and sprinkle pecans on top.

Makes 2 servings

PER SERVING: 118 calories (24 percent from fat), 3.2 g fat (0.4 g saturated, 1.6 g monounsaturated), 2 mg cholesterol, 5.9 g protein, 17.9 g carbohydrates, 1.4 g fiber, 72 mg sodium

HELPFUL HINT

- Any type of citrus-flavored fat-free, low-sugar yogurt can be used.

SHOPPING LIST

Dairy

- 1 carton fat-free, low-sugar lemon-lime yogurt

Grocery

- 1 small package pecan pieces

Produce

- 1 container fresh pineapple slices

- Pernod or other anise-flavored liqueur can be used.
- Splits or small bottles of liqueurs can be found in most liquor stores.
- Buy precut melon cubes in the produce department or at a salad bar.

SHOPPING LIST

Grocery

- 1 small bottle ouzo or Pernod

Produce

- 1 container cantaloupe cubes

Staples

- Sugar

MELON WITH OUZO

Sipping ouzo in a Greek café is a typical way to end the day in Greece. Ouzo is distilled from grapes and flavored with anise seeds. When diluted with water, it becomes cloudy and white. It's a refreshing drink on a warm evening. Here it's spooned over melon for a quick dessert.

2 cups cantaloupe cubes
½ tablespoon sugar
1 tablespoon ouzo (½ ounce)

Divide cantaloupe cubes between 2 dessert dishes. Mix sugar and ouzo together and pour over melon. Let stand while the main course is prepared and eaten. Turn the dessert a few times before serving.

Makes 2 servings

PER SERVING: 84 calories (3 percent from fat), 0.3 g fat (0.1 g saturated, 0.1 g monounsaturated), 0 mg cholesterol, 1.3 g protein, 16.2 g carbohydrates, 1.4 g fiber, 26 mg sodium

MOCHA-CREAM CAKE

The mixture of coffee and cocoa gives a rich mocha flavor to this creamy sauce. It goes well on cake, ice cream, or fruit.

- ½ cup + 1 tablespoon skim milk
- 1 teaspoon instant decaffeinated coffee
- 1 teaspoon unsweetened cocoa powder
- 1 tablespoon sugar
- ¼ teaspoon vanilla extract
- 3 tablespoons reduced-fat sour cream
- 4 teaspoons cornstarch
- 2 thin slices angel food cake (2 ounces)

Warm ½ cup milk in a saucepan. Add the coffee, cocoa powder, and sugar. Cook over low heat to dissolve coffee, cocoa, and sugar. Stir in the vanilla and sour cream. Mix cornstarch with 1 tablespoon cold skim milk and add to coffee mixture. Stir well and cook 30 seconds, or until sauce thickens. Sauce should be thickened but still a pouring consistency.

Place a slice of cake on each plate. Spoon 3 tablespoons sauce over each piece.

Makes 2 servings

PER SERVING: 180 calories (17 percent from fat), 3.4 g fat (2.1 g saturated, 0.1 g monounsaturated), 264 mg cholesterol, 5.1 g protein, 33.7 g carbohydrates, 0.8 g fiber, 264 mg sodium

HELPFUL HINTS

- Sauce may be made ahead and gently rewarmed before use. It also can be served at room temperature.
- Angel food cake can be found in the supermarket. Any low-fat cake can be substituted.

SHOPPING LIST

Dairy

- 1 small carton reduced-fat sour cream

Grocery

- 1 container unsweetened cocoa powder
- 1 small angel food cake
- 1 small bottle instant decaffeinated coffee

Staples

- Skim milk
- Vanilla extract
- Cornstarch
- Sugar

Photo on page 62.

- Whipped egg whites become soft when sugar is added. When the sugar is added to the egg whites, continue to whip the whites until stiff again.

- Peaches or nectarines can be used instead of plums.

COUNTDOWN

- Preheat oven to 350 degrees.

- Assemble ingredients.

- Microwave plums.

- Whip egg whites and complete dish.

SHOPPING LIST

Produce

- 4 plums

Staples

- Eggs

- Brown sugar

PLUM MERINGUE

The meringue covers the plums like a golden cloud. It will end your meal with a smile.

4 plums, pit removed and sliced (about 2 cups)

2 tablespoons brown sugar, divided use

2 large egg whites

Preheat oven to 350 degrees.

Place plums in a microwaveable bowl and mix with 1 tablespoon brown sugar. Microwave on high 2 minutes. Transfer to 2 ramekins or small dishes that are ovenproof (about 3½ inches in diameter and 2 inches deep).

Place the egg whites in the bowl of an electric mixer. Whip to a stiff peak. Add 1 tablespoon brown sugar and whip to stiff peak again.

Spoon egg whites into ramekins, making sure the egg whites completely cover the plums. Place ramekins in oven for 5 minutes, or until meringue is golden. Serve immediately.

Makes 2 servings

PER SERVING: 140 calories (5 percent from fat), 0.8 g fat (0.1 g saturated, 0.1 g monounsaturated), 0 mg cholesterol, 4.5 g protein, 30.5 g carbohydrates, 2.0 g fiber, 10 mg sodium

SPICED ORANGES

Cinnamon and cloves spice up orange slices for a refreshing, quick dessert.

2 medium oranges, peeled and sliced (about 1½ cups)

1 tablespoon sugar

¼ teaspoon ground cinnamon

⅛ teaspoon ground cloves

¼ cup water

1 tablespoon broken walnuts

Arrange orange slices on 2 dessert plates. Combine sugar, cinnamon, cloves, and water in a small saucepan. Bring to a boil, lower heat, and simmer 2 minutes. Pour over oranges. Sprinkle walnuts on top and serve.

Makes 2 servings

PER SERVING: 112 calories (21 percent from fat), 2.6 g fat (0.3 g saturated, 0.4 g monounsaturated), 0 mg cholesterol, 1.8 g protein, 22.5 g carbohydrates, 3.6 g fiber, 1 mg sodium

HELPFUL HINTS

- The sauce can be made ahead.
- Tangerines can be used instead of oranges.

SHOPPING LIST

Grocery

- 1 small package walnut pieces

Produce

- 2 medium oranges

Staples

- Sugar
- Ground cinnamon
- Ground cloves

- Any type of orange liqueur can be used.

Dairy

- 1 small carton whipping cream

Produce

- 1 container strawberries

Grocery

- 1 small bottle Grand Marnier

Staples

- Sugar
- Vanilla extract

STRAWBERRIES IN GRAND MARNIER

Liqueur complements the flavor of fresh fruit. The Grand Marnier adds a sweet, orange flavor to this dessert.

2 cups strawberries, hulled and washed, divided use

2 teaspoons sugar

2 tablespoons whipping cream

1 tablespoon Grand Marnier (½ ounce)

½ teaspoon vanilla extract

Slice 1 ½ cups strawberries and divide between 2 dessert dishes. Puree the remaining strawberries in a food processor and mix with the sugar, cream, Grand Marnier, and vanilla. Spoon sauce over strawberries.

Makes 2 servings

PER SERVING: 147 calories (37 percent from fat), 6.1 g fat (3.5 g saturated, 1.7 g monounsaturated), 20 mg cholesterol, 1.2 g protein, 18.9 g carbohydrates, 3.5 g fiber, 8 mg sodium

VELVETY CHOCOLATE MOUSSE

This smooth, velvety, and light-as-a-cloud mousse is made without cream or butter, so the pure chocolate flavor comes through. The secret is beating the egg whites until they are stiff, but not dry. When the beater is lifted from the bowl, peaks should stand in stiff points. When the bowl is tipped, the whites do not slide.

1½ ounces bitter chocolate

½ tablespoon unsweetened cocoa powder

1 tablespoon strong black coffee (can use instant)

3 pasteurized eggs

1½ tablespoons sugar

1 tablespoon shaved chocolate curls (optional)

FOR THE CHOCOLATE

Microwave method: Place chocolate in a microwaveable bowl and microwave on high for 30 seconds. (If it is not melted, return to the microwave for 30 seconds.) Remove, stir, and add the cocoa powder and coffee.

Stove-top method: Break chocolate into pieces and place in a bowl over a saucepan of hot water. Make sure the bottom of the bowl does not touch the water. Add the cocoa powder and coffee. Stir to blend.

TO MAKE THE MOUSSE

Separate the eggs and discard the yolks. Beat egg whites to a medium peak (the whites will form a peak but be very soft). Add the sugar and continue to beat until the whites form a stiff peak. Take a spoonful of the whites and stir it into the chocolate mixture to lighten it. Fold the chocolate mixture into the whites, making sure all of the white is incorporated. Spoon into 2 dessert dishes. If making chocolate curls, scrape the sides of room-temperature dark chocolate with a potato peeler. Sprinkle chocolate curls on top of the mousse and refrigerate until needed. The mousse is best when made 1 hour ahead. It can also be made in the morning for dessert that evening.

Makes 2 servings

PER SERVING: 193 calories (64 percent from fat), 13.7 g fat (8.1 g saturated, 4.6 g monounsaturated), 0 mg cholesterol, 8.0 g protein, 17.6 g carbohydrates, 4.2 g fiber, 10 mg sodium

Photo on back cover.

HELPFUL HINTS

- Use best-quality chocolate.
- The egg whites should be at room temperature.
- Decaffeinated or regular coffee can be used.
- This mousse has a deep chocolate flavor. For a lighter flavor, use 1 ounce of chocolate instead of 1½ ounces.
- To make chocolate curls, bring chocolate to room temperature and soften slightly with a warm hand. Scrape chocolate with potato peeler.

COUNTDOWN

- Melt chocolate and mix with cocoa and coffee.
- Whip egg whites.
- Fold mixtures together.

SHOPPING LIST

Grocery

- 1 small package bitter chocolate
- 1 container unsweetened cocoa powder

Staples

- Pasteurized eggs
- Coffee
- Sugar

COUNTDOWN

- Make sauce.
- Assemble crepes.

SHOPPING LIST

Grocery

- 1 package ready-made 7-inch crepes

Produce

- 1 container blueberries
- 1 container raspberries

Staples

- Sugar
- Cornstarch

VERY BERRY CREPES

Crepes stuffed with fresh berries make an enticing, simple dessert. You can buy ready-made crepes in most supermarkets.

1 cup blueberries, divided use

1 tablespoon sugar

1 teaspoon cornstarch

¼ cup water

1 cup raspberries

2 7-inch ready-made crepes

Reserve ½ cup blueberries. Combine sugar and cornstarch in a small saucepan. Add water and bring to a simmer. Add the remaining ½ cup blueberries and simmer 2 minutes, stirring constantly, or until sauce thickens and turns blue. Remove 3 tablespoons of sauce and set aside. Reserve several raspberries and blueberries for garnish on top of crepes. Stir remaining berries into the hot sauce. Spoon berry sauce onto the center of 2 crepes and fold the sides in to cover the berries. Drizzle reserved 3 tablespoons of sauce over top of crepes. Sprinkle reserved blueberries and raspberries on top.

Makes 2 servings

PER SERVING: 130 calories (8 percent from fat), 1.1 g fat (0.5 g saturated, 0.4 g monounsaturated), 5 mg cholesterol, 2.0 g protein, 29.8 g carbohydrates, 4.9 g fiber, 55 mg sodium

ENTERTAINING

Casual Supper for Six

Here's a casual supper you can make when friends stop by or for a Sunday night party. Fideua, Catalonian Paella, is a traditional Spanish dish and the centerpiece for this festive supper. I learned about it at a Catalonian restaurant where I noticed that the paella was made with pasta instead of rice. The chef told me it's a centuries-old dish from the Mediterranean areas of Valencia and Catalonia. Serve this colorful dish right from the paella pan or skillet.

Menu

COUNTDOWN

Two days ahead

- Shop for ingredients.

One day ahead

- Set table.
- Make Natilla.

On the day

- In the morning, make the Tomato-Basil Soup Shooter.
- 2 to 3 hours ahead, assemble salad, cover, and refrigerate until needed. Add dressing just before serving.
- ½ hour ahead, make paella. Cover to keep warm. Gently reheat on stove just before serving.

SHOPPING LIST

Deli

- 1 package chorizo sausage (¼ pound needed)

Seafood

- 1 package peeled shrimp (2 pounds needed)

Grocery

- 1 can sweetened condensed milk
- 1 can evaporated milk
- 1 small can tomato paste
- 1 package diced frozen onion
- 3 bottles clam juice
- 1 bottle dry white wine
- 1 package saffron
- 1 box orzo
- 1 package frozen petite peas
- 1 jar pimientos
- 1 jar pitted black olives

Produce

- 1½ pounds ripe tomatoes
- 1 large bunch basil
- ½ pound zucchini
- 1 pound asparagus (optional)
- 2 bags washed, ready-to-eat salad

Staples

- Eggs
- Sugar
- Cornstarch
- Olive oil
- Ground cinnamon
- Cayenne pepper
- Olive oil spray
- Garlic
- Fat-free, low-sodium chicken broth
- Low-fat olive oil and vinegar dressing
- Vanilla extract
- Salt
- Black peppercorns

HELPFUL HINT

- Drained canned low-sodium, whole tomatoes can be used if fresh ones are not ripe.

TOMATO-BASIL SOUP SHOOTER

It takes only minutes to make this cold soup in a blender or food processor. Serve it in shot glasses or small cups. Guests can drink it while standing or chatting.

1½ pounds ripe tomatoes, quartered (4¼ cups), or 4¼ cups canned low-sodium, whole tomatoes, drained

¾ cup fat-free, low-sodium chicken broth

1 cup fresh basil leaves

3½ tablespoons tomato paste

1½ tablespoons olive oil

2 medium cloves garlic, crushed

¼ teaspoon cayenne pepper

Salt and freshly ground black pepper

Place tomatoes, chicken broth, basil, tomato paste, olive oil, and garlic in a blender or food processor. Process until smooth. Add cayenne pepper and salt and pepper to taste. Process to combine flavors. Pour into a pitcher and refrigerate until needed. Bring to room temperature and pour into shot glasses or small martini glasses.

Makes 6 servings

PER SERVING: 67 calories (51 percent from fat), 3.7 g fat (0.5 g saturated, 2.6 g monounsaturated), 0 mg cholesterol, 2.1 g protein, 7.8 g carbohydrates, 2.3 g fiber, 86 mg sodium

CATALONIAN PAELLA (FIDEUA)

Olive oil spray

¼ pound chorizo sausage, diced (about 1 cup)

3 cups diced, frozen onion

6 medium cloves garlic, crushed

3 cups clam juice

2 cups dry white wine

1 teaspoon saffron

1 cup orzo

½ pound zucchini, sliced (about 3 cups)

1½ cups canned pimientos, drained and sliced

½ cup frozen petite peas

2 pounds peeled shrimp

Salt and freshly ground black pepper

Coat paella pan or large skillet with olive oil spray. Add chorizo and onion. Cook 2 minutes. Add the garlic and cook 1 minute. Add the clam juice, white wine, and saffron. Bring to a boil. Add orzo. Stir, bring back to a boil, and cook 8 minutes. If not using a nonstick pan, stir often to keep orzo from sticking. If pan becomes dry, add a little water. Add zucchini and pimiento. Cook 3 minutes. Add the peas and shrimp. Cook 2 minutes. Turn shrimp to make sure all sides are cooked. The shrimp should be pink. Add salt and pepper to taste.

Makes 6 servings

PER SERVING: 587 calories (29 percent from fat), 19.0 g fat (6.2 g saturated, 7.4 g monounsaturated), 263 mg cholesterol, 47.2 g protein, 41.7 g carbohydrates, 4.1 g fiber, 979 mg sodium

HELPFUL HINTS

- If paella becomes dry when made ahead, add more clam juice and rewarm.

- Saffron, which is sold powdered or in threads, provides a delicate, aromatic flavor. A little bit of saffron goes a long way. Turmeric or Bijol can be used instead.

- If in season, add 1 pound fresh asparagus cut into 2-inch pieces with the zucchini

- Any type of olives can be used.

OLIVE AND LETTUCE SALAD

6 cups washed, ready-to-eat salad

12 pitted black olives

6 tablespoons reduced-fat olive oil and vinegar dressing

Place lettuce in bowl, add olives, and toss with dressing.

Makes 2 servings

PER SERVING: 44 calories (67 percent from fat), 3.3 g fat (0.3 g saturated, 0.8 g monounsaturated), 0 g cholesterol, 1.2 g protein, 3.1 g carbohydrates, 1.4 g fiber, 194 mg sodium

NATILLA (SPANISH CUSTARD)

¾ cup sweetened condensed milk

¾ cup + 3 tablespoons water

¾ cup canned evaporated milk

2 egg yolks

2 tablespoons sugar

1½ tablespoons cornstarch

2 teaspoons vanilla extract

2 teaspoons ground cinnamon

Combine the condensed milk, ¾ cup water, evaporated milk, egg yolks, and sugar in a saucepan. In a cup, mix the cornstarch and 3 tablespoons water and add to the mixture. Bring to a boil. Lower heat to medium, stirring constantly with a whisk, and cook until the mixture begins to thicken and bubbles begin to appear. Remove from the heat and stir in the vanilla. Pour into 6 small ramekins or dessert bowls. Sprinkle with cinnamon and refrigerate until needed. Bring to room temperature before serving.

Makes 6 servings

PER SERVING: 194 calories (28 percent from fat), 6.1 g fat (3.4 g saturated, 1.7 g monounsaturated), 88 mg cholesterol, 5.1 g protein, 29.4 g carbohydrates, 0.4 g fiber, 69 mg sodium

HELPFUL HINT

- Be sure to stir constantly to keep the natilla from burning on the bottom of the saucepan.

Barbecue Buffet

Bring out the barbecue or use a stove-top grill for this flavor-packed buffet. Most of the recipes can be made a day ahead. The grilled foods can be cooked just before serving or cooked 2 hours ahead and kept warm in a 150-degree oven.

Menu

Grilled Five-Spice Shrimp on Skewers 212

Barbecued Korean Chicken 213

Sweet Potato Salad 214

Broccoli Slaw 215

Sorbet Cups 215

COUNTDOWN

Two days ahead

- Shop for ingredients.

One day ahead

- Set table.
- Marinate chicken.
- Make broccoli slaw.
- Make potato salad.

On the day

- In the morning, marinate shrimp, place on skewers, and refrigerate.
- 3 hours ahead, place dessert bowls in the freezer.
- 1 hour ahead, scoop sorbet into the bowls and return to freezer. Add chocolate just before serving.
- ½ hour ahead, grill chicken. Place in 150-degree oven to keep warm. Soak skewers for shrimp.
- When guests arrive, grill shrimp.

SHOPPING LIST

Meat and Seafood

- 1 package 24-count peeled shrimp (1 pound needed)
- Boneless, skinless chicken thighs (2½ pounds needed)

Grocery

- 1 container five-spice powder
- 6-inch wooden skewers (24 needed)
- 1 bottle rice wine vinegar
- 1 small container sesame seeds
- 1 bottle low-sodium soy sauce
- 1 bottle apple cider vinegar

Produce

- 1 small piece fresh ginger
- 1½ pounds sweet potatoes
- 1 medium green bell pepper
- 1 small head frisee lettuce
- 1 bunch flat-leaf parsley
- 1 large tomato
- 1 bag washed, ready-to-eat shredded broccoli slaw
- 1 large container raspberry sorbet
- 1 small package semisweet chocolate
- 1 small package chocolate chip cookies (look for cookies that are ⅓ ounce or 10 grams each)

Staples

- Sugar
- Garlic
- Red onion
- Dijon mustard
- Olive oil
- Reduced-fat mayonnaise
- Salt
- Black peppercorns

The recipes for this party contain 880 calories with 31 percent of calories from fat.

HELPFUL HINTS

- Five-spice powder can be found in the spice section of the super-market.

- Soak skewers in cold water at least 30 minutes before threading shrimp.

- To keep the shrimp from rolling on their skewer when they are turned over, thread the skewer through the tail and then through the thick end.

- Use small wooden skewers and serve the shrimp right on the skewer.

- The shrimp can be coated with the spice mixture, threaded onto the skewers, and kept in the refrigerator until ready to cook. Bring to room temperature before grilling.

GRILLED FIVE-SPICE SHRIMP ON SKEWERS

4 teaspoons sugar

2 teaspoons salt

3 teaspoons five-spice powder

1 teaspoon freshly ground black pepper

1 pound 24-count peeled shrimp

Prepare a barbecue grill or preheat a gas grill. Have 24 small wooden skewers (about 6 inches each) ready.

Mix sugar, salt, five-spice powder, and black pepper together. Toss the shrimp in the mixture, making sure all of the shrimp are coated. Thread one shrimp onto each skewer. Place on grill and cook 1 minute, turn, and grill 1 minute.

Makes 6 servings

PER SERVING: 92 calories (18 percent from fat), 1.9 g fat (0.3 g saturated, 0.5 g monounsaturated), 115 mg cholesterol, 16.0 g protein, 2.6 g carbohydrates, 0.6 g fiber, 888 mg sodium

BARBECUED KOREAN CHICKEN

Photo on page 64.

2½ pounds boneless, skinless chicken thighs

½ cup low-sodium soy sauce

½ cup rice wine vinegar

4 medium cloves garlic, crushed

4 teaspoons Dijon mustard

2 teaspoons chopped fresh ginger

Dash of freshly ground black pepper

3 tablespoons sesame seeds, for garnish

Prepare a barbecue grill or preheat a gas grill.

Place chicken thighs in a zip-top plastic bag. Add the soy sauce, vinegar, garlic, mustard, ginger, and black pepper. Seal the bag and gently shake to combine ingredients. Marinate at least 15 minutes, turn the bag over, and marinate at least 15 minutes longer.

Meanwhile, add sesame seeds to a small non-stick skillet. Heat over medium for 1 to 2 minutes, or until slightly golden, tossing continuously. Do not let them turn dark brown. Remove from heat and set aside.

Remove chicken from marinade and reserve marinade. Pat chicken dry with a paper towel. Place on grill about 6 inches from the heat. Barbecue 5 minutes, turn, and cook 3 minutes longer. A meat thermometer should read 180 degrees.

Makes 6 servings

PER SERVING: 270 calories (32 percent from fat), 9.5 g fat (2.1 g saturated, 2.3 g monounsaturated), 153 mg cholesterol, 40.4 g protein, 4.4 g carbohydrates, 0.2 g fiber, 907 mg sodium

HELPFUL HINTS

- Boneless, skinless chicken thighs can be found in the meat case of the supermarket.

- A quick way to chop ginger is to grate it without peeling.

- White vinegar diluted with a little water can be used instead of rice wine vinegar.

- The chicken can be placed in the marinade the day before or 30 minutes before cooking.

- The sesame seeds can be browned the day before.

Photo on page 64.

HELPFUL HINTS

- Any type of lettuce leaves can be used as the base for the salad.
- Curly parsley can be used instead of flat-leaf parsley.
- If made a day ahead, taste for seasoning. The potatoes will absorb the seasoning and may need more salt and pepper.

1½ pounds sweet potatoes

¼ cup apple cider vinegar

2 tablespoons Dijon mustard

3 tablespoons olive oil

1 cup diced red onion

1 cup diced green bell pepper

Salt and freshly ground black pepper

½ head frisee lettuce

¼ cup chopped, fresh flat-leaf parsley

1 large tomato

Wash and peel potatoes and cut into 1-inch pieces. Place in a saucepan, cover with cold water, and place over high heat. Cover with a lid, bring to a boil, and cook 10 minutes, or until potatoes are cooked through. Meanwhile, whisk vinegar and mustard together in a large serving bowl. Add the olive oil and whisk until smooth. Remove 2 tablespoons dressing to a small bowl and set aside. Add onion, bell pepper, and salt and pepper to taste.

When potatoes are cooked, drain and add to the dressing while they are still warm. Toss. Taste for seasoning and add salt and pepper, if needed.

Layer frisee leaves on a serving platter. Spoon potato salad onto frisee. Sprinkle chopped parsley on top. Cut tomato into thin wedges. Place around edge of platter. Spoon reserved dressing over the tomatoes.

Makes 6 servings

PER SERVING: 194 calories (33 percent from fat), 7.2 g fat (1.0 g saturated, 5.1 g monounsaturated), 0 mg cholesterol, 3.7 g protein, 30.8 g carbohydrates, 5.8 g fiber, 127 mg sodium

BROCCOLI SLAW

- 5 tablespoons reduced-fat mayonnaise
- 6 tablespoons apple cider vinegar
- 2 teaspoons sugar
- Salt and freshly ground black pepper
- 6 cups washed, ready-to-eat shredded broccoli slaw
- ½ medium red onion, sliced (1 cup)

Mix mayonnaise, vinegar, sugar, and salt and pepper to taste together in a medium-size bowl. Add broccoli slaw and onion and toss well. Taste. Add more salt and pepper as needed. Let sit 30 minutes and toss again.

Makes 6 servings

PER SERVING: 85 calories (47 percent from fat), 4.4 g fat (0.7 g saturated, 1.2 g monounsaturated), 4 mg cholesterol, 2.9 g protein, 10.6 g carbohydrates, 3.0 g fiber, 125 mg sodium

Photo on page 64.

HELPFUL HINTS

- If prepared shredded broccoli slaw is not available, use prepared shredded cabbage slaw.
- This can be made a day ahead.

SORBET CUPS

- 3 cups raspberry sorbet
- ½ cup chocolate curls (nuggets) (2 ounces)
- 6 small chocolate chip cookies

Scoop sorbet into dessert bowls and sprinkle curls on top. Serve on a dish with a cookie.

Makes 6 servings

PER SERVING: 171 calories (30 percent from fat), 5.7 g fat (2.9 g saturated, 2.3 g monounsaturated), 0 mg cholesterol, 1.1 g protein, 31.5 g carbohydrates, 2.1 g fiber, 35 mg sodium

Photo on page 64.

HELPFUL HINTS

- Look for medium-size cookies about ⅓ ounce or 10 grams each.
- Place dessert bowls in the freezer before spooning the sorbet into them. This will keep the sorbet from pooling or starting to melt around the edges.
- The bowls can be filled with the sorbet and placed in the freezer until needed. Add the chocolate just before serving.
- Use a martini glass instead of a dessert bowl for an attractive presentation.

Dinner Party for Six

Here's a menu for those times when you want to serve a special dinner for friends. With these recipes, you can enjoy your guests and you won't have to spend days preparing for the party. Best of all, you won't feel guilty or break the calorie bank. You'll be serving great food that's healthful, too.

Menu

Tapenade on Toast 218

Butterflied Leg of Lamb 219

Cheese-Crusted Potatoes 220

Pear, Romaine, and Radicchio Salad with Pomegranate Dressing 221

Mixed Fruit Tart 222

COUNTDOWN

Two days ahead

- Shop for food.

One day ahead

- Set table.
- Marinate lamb.
- Mix salad dressing.
- Make fruit tart crust.

On the day

- Complete the pie recipe in the morning.
- Several hours ahead, make tapenade.
- 2 hours ahead, sear lamb in broiler, then place in 200-degree oven.
- Make potatoes and leave, covered, on stove top.
- 1 hour ahead, complete salad.
- Just before serving, gently warm the potatoes over low heat while you slice the lamb.

SHOPPING LIST

Dairy

- 1 package reduced-fat, shredded sharp Cheddar cheese
- 1 container fat-free, low-sugar vanilla yogurt

Meat

- Butterflied leg of lamb (2½ pounds needed)

Grocery

- 1 jar olive tapenade
- 1 bottle pomegranate juice
- 1 box gelatin
- 1 small box low-fat granola
- 1 small package graham cracker crumbs

Produce

- 2 lemons
- 1 bunch fresh rosemary
- 2½ pounds red potatoes
- 1 bunch scallions
- 1 bag washed, ready-to-eat baby romaine leaves
- 1 small head radicchio
- 2 ripe pears
- 1 container strawberries
- 2 ripe peaches
- 1 container blueberries

Staples

- Whole wheat bread
- Confectioners' sugar
- Olive oil
- Canola oil
- Garlic
- Fat-free, low-sodium chicken broth
- Olive oil spray
- Low-fat olive oil and vinegar dressing
- Salt
- Black peppercorns

The recipes for this party contain 804 calories with 34 percent of calories from fat.

HELPFUL HINT

- Olive tapenade is made with ripe olives, olive oil, lemon juice, and seasonings. There are several brands available in the supermarket.

TAPENADE ON TOAST

6 tablespoons olive tapenade

6 slices whole wheat bread, crusts removed and toasted

Spread tapenade over toasted bread and cut into triangles. Arrange on a platter and serve. Can be made several hours ahead.

Makes 6 servings

PER SERVING: 104 calories (41 percent from fat), 4.7 g fat (0.8 g saturated, 0.5 g monounsaturated), 0 mg cholesterol, 2.7 g protein, 13.9 g carbohydrates, 1.9 g fiber, 298 mg sodium

BUTTERFLIED LEG OF LAMB

Butterflied leg of lamb is easy to cook and serve. This method of searing the lamb and then placing it in a 200-degree oven lets you prepare most of it in advance. It slowly cooks on its own while guests arrive. It will even hold for an hour if some guests are late.

6 tablespoons olive oil

4 tablespoons lemon juice

4 medium cloves garlic, crushed

1 tablespoon fresh rosemary leaves or 2 teaspoons dried

2½ pounds butterflied leg of lamb, visible fat removed

Mix olive oil, lemon juice, garlic, and rosemary together in a large, zip-top plastic bag. Add the lamb and seal. Let marinate in the refrigerator at least 1 hour, turning once during that time, or marinate overnight, if time permits.

Preheat broiler. Remove lamb from marinade and pat dry with a paper towel. Line a baking tray with foil and place lamb on tray. Broil 5 minutes per side. Remove from broiler, baste with marinade, and place in a 200-degree oven for 1 to 2 hours. Continue to baste 2 to 3 times while lamb is in the oven. A meat thermometer will read 125 degrees for rare, 130 degrees for medium.

Carve lamb into slanting slices across the grain. Spoon pan juices over the meat.

Makes 6 servings

PER SERVING: 296 calories (44 percent from fat), 14.5 g fat (4.2 g saturated, 7.4 g monounsaturated), 120 mg cholesterol, 38.3 g protein, 0.5 g carbohydrates, 0.1 g fiber, 120 mg sodium

HELPFUL HINTS

- Some markets sell leg of lamb already boned. If not, ask the butcher to bone it for you.

- A 6- to 7-pound leg of lamb will serve 10 to 12 people. Ask for half a leg or cut the full leg in half and freeze one half for another meal.

- Use a zip-top plastic bag to marinate the lamb. You only need to flip the bag over to turn the meat. It also saves washing an extra bowl.

- The leg of lamb can be seared on a barbecue grill instead of under the broiler. Place it in the oven after it has been seared.

- Slice the potatoes in a food processor fitted with a slicing blade.

- Cook the potatoes in an attractive stove-to-table skillet for an easy, attractive presentation.

- Potatoes can be gently rewarmed on a low flame.

CHEESE-CRUSTED POTATOES

2½ pounds red potatoes, washed, not peeled, and sliced about ¼ inch thick

Salt and freshly ground black pepper

1¼ cups fat-free, low-sodium chicken broth

2 teaspoons olive oil

½ cup reduced-fat, shredded sharp Cheddar cheese (2 ounces)

2 scallions, washed and sliced

Place a layer of potatoes in a 12-inch skillet. Sprinkle with salt and pepper to taste. Continue to layer the potatoes and season with salt and pepper. Mix the chicken broth and olive oil together and add to the skillet. Bring to a simmer, cover, and cook gently, 10 minutes. Uncover and cook until the liquid has evaporated, about 2 to 3 minutes. Add salt and pepper to taste. Sprinkle cheese over top and cover for 1 to 2 minutes to melt cheese. Sprinkle with scallions and serve in the skillet, or remove potatoes to a serving platter and then sprinkle with scallions.

Makes 6 servings

PER SERVING: 184 calories (11 percent from fat), 2.3 g fat (0.7 g saturated, 1.3 g monounsaturated), 2 mg cholesterol, 7.1 g protein, 35.0 g carbohydrates 2.6 g fiber, 187 mg sodium

PEAR, ROMAINE, AND RADICCHIO SALAD WITH POMEGRANATE DRESSING

4 cups washed, ready-to-eat baby romaine leaves

3 cups radicchio, washed and leaves torn into bite-size pieces

2 tablespoons pomegranate juice

6 tablespoons low-fat olive oil and vinegar dressing

2 ripe pears

Place romaine and radicchio leaves in a salad bowl. In a small bowl, mix pomegranate juice and dressing together. Wash, core, and slice pears. Toss pears in the dressing, then remove and add pears to salad bowl. Set aside the dressing. Just before serving, add reserved dressing to salad and toss.

Makes 6 servings

PER SERVING: 71 calories (33 percent from fat), 2.6 g fat (0.2 g saturated, 0 g monounsaturated), 0 mg cholesterol, 1.5 g protein, 11.9 g carbohydrates, 2.7 g fiber, 120 mg sodium

HELPFUL HINTS

- Pomegranate juice can be found in most supermarkets. If unavailable, use a tart fruit juice.

- The dressing can be mixed a day ahead.

- The salad can be placed in an attractive salad bowl, covered, and refrigerated in the morning. The pears should be added about 1 hour in advance of serving.

Photo on page 63.

HELPFUL HINTS

- The crust can be made a day ahead and refrigerated.

- The tart can be made in the morning.

- Make sure the yogurt is at room temperature before adding the gelatin.

MIXED FRUIT TART

1 tablespoon gelatin

2 tablespoons water

½ cup low-fat granola

½ cup graham cracker crumbs

3 tablespoons canola oil
  Olive oil spray

1 cup fat-free, low-sugar vanilla yogurt

1 cup sliced strawberries

1 cup sliced ripe peaches

1 cup blueberries

3 tablespoons confectioners' sugar

Mix gelatin and water together in a small glass mixing cup and set aside. Remove yogurt from refrigerator and allow to come to room temperature.

Place granola, graham cracker crumbs, and oil in the bowl of a food processor. Process until oil is mixed into the dry ingredients. Coat a 7- to 8-inch pie plate with olive oil spray and press crumbs into place. Refrigerate while preparing other ingredients.

Place the mixing cup with gelatin in a sauce-pan. Fill the saucepan with water to reach three-fourths the way up the side of the cup Heat water to dissolve gelatin, about 2 minutes. Once the gelatin is clear, stir it into the yogurt. Remove the pie plate from the refrigerator and spread the yogurt mixture over the bottom. Return to the refrigerator for 5 minutes.

Remove from refrigerator and spread strawberries and peach slices over the yogurt. Sprinkle the blueberries on top and refrigerate. Remove about 15 minutes before serving. Sprinkle sugar on top and serve.

Makes 8 servings

PER SERVING: 149 calories (39 percent from fat), 6.4 g fat (1.0 g saturated, 4.1 g monounsaturated), 1 mg cholesterol, 3.7 g protein, 20.0 g carbohydrates, 1.8 g fiber, 89 mg sodium

Sunday Brunch

Greet your guests with a colorful blueberry smoothie for this easy-to-prepare Sunday brunch. The beauty of this brunch is that the Tortilla Omelets and Almond Chicken Salad can be prepared the day before.

Menu

Blueberry Smoothie 226

Tortilla Omelets 227

Almond Chicken Salad 228

Tropical Fruit Salad with Pomegranate Cream 229

COUNTDOWN

Two days ahead

- Shop for ingredients.

One day ahead

- Make Tortilla Omelets.
- Make Almond Chicken Salad.
- Cut fruit and store in plastic containers.
- Whip cream and store in a covered container in the refrigerator.

On the day

- Prepare ingredients for Blueberry Smoothie.
- Complete Tropical Fruit Salad and store in refrigerator.

Just before guests arrive

- Warm omelets.
- Make smoothies

SHOPPING LIST

Dairy

- 2 cartons nonfat, light blueberry yogurt
- 1 small carton heavy whipping cream

Deli

- 1 package lean ham (¾ pound needed)
- 1 package roasted chicken breast, skin and bones removed (½ pounds needed)

Grocery

- 1 bottle pomegranate juice
- 1 small package sliced almonds
- 1 bottle chipotle powder
- 1 package whole grain dinner rolls
- 1 jar roasted red peppers
- 1 package 10-inch whole wheat tortillas

Produce

- 1 container blueberries
- 1 ripe mango
- 1 small papaya
- 1 container fresh pineapple cubes
- 1 small bunch seedless grapes
- 1 small fennel bulb with leaves
- 2 medium tomatoes
- 1 small bunch fresh mint
- 1 small bunch arugula

Staples

- Eggs
- Sugar
- Ground cinnamon
- Reduced-fat mayonnaise
- Salt
- Black peppercorns
- Olive oil spray

The recipes for this party contain 874 calories with 33 percent of calories from fat.

HELPFUL HINTS

- Prepare the ingredients for this smoothie and make it in a blender just before needed.

- It's best to make the smoothie in two batches to keep the blender from overflowing.

- If smoothie separates before serving, return to blender for a few seconds.

BLUEBERRY SMOOTHIE

1½ cups blueberries

2 cups nonfat, light blueberry yogurt

1 tablespoon sugar

1½ teaspoons ground cinnamon

1½ cups water

2½ cups ice cubes

Place blueberries, yogurt, sugar, cinnamon, and water in a blender. Blend about 30 seconds or until smooth. Pour out half into a pitcher and add half the ice cubes to the blender. Blend 30 seconds or until thick. Divide evenly among three 8-ounce glasses. Pour mixture from the pitcher into the blender and add remaining ice cubes. Blend 30 seconds or until thick. Pour into the 8-ounce glasses.

Makes six 6-ounce servings

PER SERVING: 75 calories (3 percent from fat), 0.3 g fat (0.1 g saturated, 0.1 g monounsaturated), 2 mg cholesterol, 5.0 g protein, 13.9 g carbohydrates, 1.3 g fiber, 66 mg sodium

TORTILLA OMELETS

6 whole eggs

12 egg whites

12 tablespoons water

1 teaspoon chipotle powder

Salt and freshly ground black pepper

6 10-inch whole wheat tortillas

Olive oil spray

¾ pound shredded lean ham

½ cup drained, sliced roasted red peppers

12 large arugula leaves

Mix together whole eggs, egg whites, water, chipotle powder, and salt and pepper to taste. Heat a 10-inch nonstick skillet on medium-high heat. Add the tortillas one at a time for about 30 seconds to warm. Place them on a plate and cover with another plate or foil to keep warm.

Coat the skillet with olive oil spray and pour ½ cup of the egg mixture into the skillet, tipping the skillet as you pour so egg covers the bottom of the skillet. As the egg cooks, scrape it toward the middle along the edges and let the egg run into the holes. Continue to scrape around the edges until all of the runny egg is cooked. This takes about 20 seconds. Sprinkle ham all over the top. Slide the omelet onto one of the tortillas. Place 1¼ tablespoons roasted peppers and 2 arugula leaves on top of the ham. Roll up the tortilla and press gently to help it hold together. Continue to make the remaining 5 omelets in the same way. The dish can be made ahead to this point. Cover and refrigerate.

To serve, warm 5 minutes in a 350-degree oven or toaster oven. Cut in half on a diagonal and arrange on platter.

Makes 6 servings

PER SERVING: 337 calories (32 percent from fat), 12.0 g fat (3.5 g saturated, 3.4 g monounsaturated), 243 mg cholesterol, 29.0 g protein, 25.6 g carbohydrates, 3.4 g fiber, 964 mg sodium

HELPFUL HINTS

- If making these in advance, rewarm them in a 300 degree oven for 15 minutes.
- Chipotle powder can be found in the spice section.

- Any type of cooked chicken breast can be used. Remove the skin and bones.

- Use feathery fennel leaves as a garnish.

- A quick way to chop fennel leaves is to snip them with a scissors.

- Celery can be substituted for the fennel.

ALMOND CHICKEN SALAD

¾ cup reduced-fat mayonnaise

¾ cup warm water

1½ cups seedless grapes, cut in half

1 cup coarsely chopped fennel

1½ pounds roasted chicken breast, skin and bones removed, cut into ½-inch pieces

2 tablespoons sliced almonds

Salt and freshly ground black pepper

2 medium tomatoes, cut into wedges (about 1½ cups)

2 tablespoons chopped fennel leaves

6 whole grain dinner rolls

Mix mayonnaise and water together in a large bowl. Add the grapes, fennel, chicken, and almonds. Toss well. Add salt and pepper to taste. Place in shallow serving dish and add tomato wedges around the edge. Sprinkle fennel leaves on top. Serve with dinner rolls.

Makes 6 servings

PER SERVING: 368 calories (35 percent from fat), 14.2 g fat (2.4 g saturated, 4.5 g monounsaturated), 74 mg cholesterol, 31.6 g protein, 29.2 g carbohydrates, 4.4 g fiber, 545 mg sodium

TROPICAL FRUIT SALAD WITH POMEGRANATE CREAM

1 ripe mango, cut into
½-inch cubes (1 cup)

1 small papaya, cut into
½-inch cubes (1 cup)

1 cup pineapple, cut into
½-inch cubes

6 tablespoons heavy
whipping cream

2 tablespoons
pomegranate juice

6 small sprigs mint leaves

Cut fruit cubes over a bowl to catch their juices. Mix the fruit together and spoon into 6-ounce wine glasses with their juice. Whip the cream and when stiff, whip in the pomegranate juice. Place a dollop of 2 tablespoons whipped cream on top of each glass of fruit.

Makes 6 servings

PER SERVING: 94 calories (54 percent from fat), 5.7 g fat (3.5 g saturated, 1.6 g monounsaturated), 20 mg cholesterol, 0.7 g protein, 12.9 g carbohydrates, 1.2 g fiber, 9 mg sodium

HELPFUL HINTS

- Any type of fruit can be used.
- Make sure fruit is ripe.
- Pomegranate juice can be found in most supermarkets. Grape juice can be substituted.
- The fruit can be cut and the cream whipped the day before. Assemble the dessert about 3 hours before serving.

Weeknight Celebration

Weeknight celebrations are a breeze with these do-it-yourself Tex-Mex fajitas. Serve with an array of colorful vegetables and let everyone help themselves to their favorite fillers.

Menu

Salsa Guacamole 232

Steak Fajitas 233

Layered Black Bean and Corn Salad 234

Tipsy Chocolate Pineapple 235

COUNTDOWN
Two days ahead

- Shop for ingredients.

One day ahead

- Prepare fajita ingredients.
- Assemble Layered Black Bean and Corn Salad. Do not add dressing.
- Make chocolate sauce for Tipsy Chocolate Pineapple.

On the day

- Make Salsa Guacamole.
- Make Tipsy Chocolate Pineapple.

Just before guests arrive

- Pour dressing over salad.
- Make fajitas and keep warm in 250-degree oven.

SHOPPING LIST
Meat

- 1 package sirloin steak (1½ pounds needed)

Grocery

- 1 bottle tomato salsa
- 1 bottle fajita marinade
- 1 package 10-inch whole wheat tortillas
- 1 can black beans
- 1 package frozen corn kernels
- 1 small package semisweet chocolate
- 1 small bottle tequila
- 1 container ground cumin

Produce

- 1 Haas-style avocado
- 1 small bunch celery
- 1 package snow peas
- 1 package peeled baby carrots
- 1 medium red pepper
- 1 medium yellow pepper
- 2 medium tomatoes
- 1 bunch cilantro
- 1 package shredded lettuce
- 1 container fresh pineapple cubes

Staples

- Red onion
- Onion
- Garlic
- Balsamic vinegar
- Canola oil
- Olive oil
- Sugar
- Hot-pepper sauce
- Vanilla extract
- Salt
- Black peppercorns

The recipes for this party contain 935 calories with 32 percent of calories from fat.

HELPFUL HINTS

- To ripen an avocado, keep it in a paper bag in a warm spot.

- To keep guacamole from turning brown, place in a bowl and wrap with plastic wrap, pressing the wrap directly onto the guacamole. It will keep several hours in the refrigerator this way.

- Green beans, broccoli florets, and cauliflower florets can be used for dipping.

SALSA GUACAMOLE

1 6-ounce Haas-style ripe avocado, cut into cubes

½ cup tomato salsa

2 cups celery sticks

2 cups trimmed snow peas

2 cups peeled baby carrots

Mix avocado and tomato salsa together by hand or in a food processor. Place on a tray and arrange the vegetables around it for dipping.

Makes 6 servings

PER SERVING: 87 calories (49 percent from fat), 4.7 g fat (0.7 g saturated, 2.9 g monounsaturated), 0 mg cholesterol, 2.2 g protein, 11.0 g carbohydrates, 4.7 g fiber, 146 mg sodium

STEAK FAJITAS

1½ pounds sirloin steak, visible fat removed, cut into ¼-inch strips

1 cup bottled fajita marinade

6 10-inch whole wheat tortillas

1 tablespoon canola oil, divided use

3 cups sliced red onion

4 medium cloves garlic, crushed

½ medium red bell pepper, sliced (about 1 cup)

½ medium yellow bell pepper, sliced (about 1 cup)

2 ripe medium tomatoes, diced (about 2 cups)

1 cup fresh cilantro

Preheat oven to 350 degrees.

Place steak strips in marinade. Tightly wrap tortillas in foil and place in the preheated oven for 15 minutes. Remove and leave wrapped. Lower oven to 250 degrees.

Heat ½ tablespoon oil in a nonstick skillet over high heat. Add the onion and garlic. Cook 2 minutes and remove to an ovenproof bowl. Add the red and yellow peppers to the skillet. Cook 2 minutes and place in another ovenproof bowl. Place both bowls in the oven to keep warm. Add the steak and marinade to the skillet. Cook 3 minutes, or until the steak is slightly pink. Remove to another ovenproof bowl and place in the oven. Return the covered tortillas to the oven.

To serve, place tomatoes and cilantro in separate bowls. Place all of the bowls on a serving tray with the tortillas. Bring to the table and let everyone fill their own.

Makes 6 servings

PER SERVING: 428 calories (22 percent from fat), 10.5 g fat (3.1 g saturated, 4.0 g monounsaturated), 68 mg cholesterol, 30.4 g protein, 54.8 g carbohydrates, 6.6 g fiber, 1,030 mg sodium

HELPFUL HINTS

- This recipe can be made 30 minutes ahead and kept warm in a 250-degree oven.
- Look for a prepared fajita marinade that has about 20 calories per tablespoon.

● To quickly defrost corn,
place in a microwave
oven for 2 minutes. Or
place in a small pan of
boiling water for 1
minute.

LAYERED BLACK BEAN AND CORN SALAD

4 tablespoons balsamic
vinegar

3 tablespoons olive oil

2 teaspoons ground
cumin

Several drops hot-
pepper sauce

Salt and freshly ground
black pepper

3 cups shredded lettuce

2 cups black beans,
rinsed and drained

1 cup diced onion

2 cups frozen corn
kernels, defrosted

½ cup chopped fresh
cilantro

Mix vinegar, olive oil, cumin, and hot sauce together in a small bowl. Add salt and pepper to taste. Place lettuce in a salad bowl. Spoon black beans over lettuce. Scatter the onion on top of the beans. Spoon corn over onion. Pour the dressing over the salad and scatter cilantro on top. Toss well.

Makes 2 servings

PER SERVING: 204 calories (33 percent from fat), 7.4 g fat (1.0 g saturated, 5.2 g monounsaturated), 0 mg cholesterol, 7.4 g protein, 30.0 g carbohydrates, 5.5 g fiber, 10 mg sodium

TIPSY CHOCOLATE PINEAPPLE

- 4 ounces semisweet chocolate
- 3 tablespoons sugar
- ½ cup water
- 1 teaspoon vanilla extract
- 6 cups fresh pineapple cubes
- 2 ounces tequila

Break chocolate into small pieces and place in a saucepan with the sugar and water. Bring to a simmer and melt the chocolate. Continue to simmer until the sauce thickens slightly, about 2 to 3 minutes. Stir in the vanilla. Place the pineapple cubes in a bowl and add the tequila. Toss well. Divide the pineapple cubes among 6 martini glasses, including the tequila. Drizzle the chocolate sauce over the pineapple.

Makes 6 servings

PER SERVING: 225 calories (44 percent from fat), 11.0 g fat (6.1 g saturated, 3.5 g monounsaturated), 0 mg cholesterol, 2.5 g protein, 30.8 g carbohydrates, 4.8 g fiber, 5 mg sodium

HELPFUL HINTS

- Be careful melting the chocolate. Bring it to a gentle simmer and do not boil.
- This dessert can be served in any type of dessert bowl or glass.

Family Holiday

There's no need to spend all day in the kitchen for this family holiday dinner. A tangy, Dijon mustard sauce flavors juicy, tender pork and the Frozen Yogurt Pie will please the whole family.

Menu

Black Bean Pate 238

Dijon Pork 239

Shredded Carrots and Zucchini 240

Orzo and Sun-Dried Tomatoes 240

Frozen Yogurt Pie 241

COUNTDOWN

Two days ahead

- Shop for ingredients.
- Make Frozen Yogurt Pie.

One day ahead

- Make Orzo and Sun-Dried Tomatoes.

On the day

- Make Dijon Pork.
- Make Shredded Carrots and Zucchini.

Just before guests arrive

- Assemble Black Bean Pate.

Fifteen minutes before dessert

- Remove pie from the freezer.

SHOPPING LIST

Dairy

- 1 carton cream
- 1 carton frozen, low-sugar yogurt

Meat

- 1 package pork tenderloin (2¼ pounds needed)

Grocery

- 1 bottle black bean pate
- 1 box orzo
- 1 jar sun-dried tomatoes packed in oil
- 1 box chocolate graham crackers
- 2 ounces dark chocolate
- 1 small package raisins
- 1 small container dried tarragon

Produce

- 2 large heads Belgian endive
- 1 container grape tomatoes
- 2 limes
- 2 lemons
- 1 bunch fresh basil
- 1 bag carrots
- Zucchini

Staples

- Dijon mustard
- Olive oil spray
- Vegetable oil spray
- Olive oil
- Salt
- Black peppercorns

The recipes for this party contain 763 calories with 39 percent of calories from fat.

HELPFUL HINTS

- If black bean pate is unavailable, use a red bean dip or humus.
- The endive leaves only need to be wiped with a damp cloth. They will turn brown if washed under water.

BLACK BEAN PATE

12 large Belgian endive leaves

12 tablespoons bottled black bean pate

 1 cup grape tomatoes

To make spears, remove the largest leaves from the endive and wipe with a damp cloth. Place 1 tablespoon black bean pate in the wide portion of the leaf near the end. Arrange the leaves side-by-side on a platter with the filled section toward the middle. Place the tomatoes in a group at the end of the wide portion.

Makes 6 servings

PER SERVING: 40 calories (2 percent from fat), 0.1 g fat (0 g saturated, 0 g monounsaturated), 0 mg cholesterol, 1.6 g protein, 5.6 g carbohydrates, 2.0 g fiber, 123 mg sodium

DIJON PORK

For this recipe, the pork is butterflied for faster cooking. It is easy to do, or ask the butcher to butterfly it for you.

2¼ pounds pork tenderloin

3 tablespoons Dijon mustard

6 tablespoons cream

Olive oil spray

Salt and freshly ground black pepper

Remove fat from pork. Cut pork almost in half lengthwise and open like a book. Cut pork in half crosswise to make 2 portions. Mix the mustard and cream together and set aside. Coat a large nonstick skillet with olive oil spray. Place over medium-high heat and add the pork. Cook 5 minutes, turn, add salt and pepper to taste to the cooked side, and cook 3 minutes longer. A meat thermometer should read 160 degrees. Remove pork to a plate. Add the sauce to the skillet and stir to dissolve brown bits in skillet. Spoon sauce over pork.

Makes 6 servings

PER SERVING: 274 calories (43 percent from fat), 13.1 g fat (5.7 g saturated, 4.4 g monounsaturated), 128 mg cholesterol, 36.3 g protein, 1.0 g carbohydrates, 0.3 g fiber, 174 mg sodium

HELPFUL HINTS

- Boneless pork chops can be substituted for pork tenderloin.

- Cook pork until a meat thermometer reads 160 degrees.

- The carrots and zucchini
  can be cooked in a
  microwave oven.
- 1 teaspoon dried
  tarragon leaves can be
  used instead of fresh
  tarragon. Make sure the
  leaves are still green, not
  gray, in the bottle.
- The carrots and zucchini
  can be shredded in a
  food processor fitted
  with a shredding blade.

SHREDDED CARROTS AND ZUCCHINI

1½ tablespoons lemon
    juice

2 tablespoons olive oil

1 tablespoon fresh
    tarragon leaves

3 cups shredded carrots

3 cups shredded zucchini

½ cup raisins

    Salt and freshly ground
    black pepper

Mix lemon juice, olive oil, and tarragon together and set aside. Bring a saucepan filled with water to a boil. Add the carrots and zucchini and boil 3 minutes. Drain and place in a serving bowl. Add the raisins, reserved sauce, and salt and pepper to taste. Toss well.

Makes 6 servings

PER SERVING: 111 calories (39 percent from fat), 4.8 g fat (0.7 g saturated, 3.3 g monounsaturated), 0 mg cholesterol, 1.6 g protein, 17.6 g carbohydrates, 3.4 g fiber, 26 mg sodium

- Be sure to drain the sun-
  dried tomatoes.
- Orzo is a rice-shaped
  pasta. Any type of short-
  cut pasta can be used.
- This can be made ahead
  and rewarmed in a
  300-degree oven for
  15 minutes. If made
  ahead, add the basil just
  before serving.
- A quick way to chop basil
  is to snip the leaves with
  a scissors.

ORZO AND SUN-DRIED TOMATOES

2 cups orzo

2 tablespoons lime juice

2 tablespoons olive oil

1 cup sun-dried tomatoes
    in oil

    Salt and freshly ground
    black pepper

½ cup chopped fresh
    basil leaves

Bring a large saucepan filled with water to a boil. Add the orzo and bring back to a boil. Cook 8 minutes, or until orzo is done. Drain and place in a serving bowl. Drizzle with lime juice and olive oil. Drain sun-dried tomatoes, cut into small pieces, and add to the orzo. Add salt and pepper to taste. Toss well. Sprinkle basil on top.

Makes 6 servings

PER SERVING: 147 calories (45 percent from fat), 7.4 g fat (1.0 g saturated, 4.9 g monounsaturated), 0 mg cholesterol, 3.3 g protein, 18.1 g carbohydrates, 2.0 g fiber, 49 mg sodium

FROZEN YOGURT PIE

Vegetable oil spray

½ cup chocolate graham cracker crumbs

3 cups frozen, low-sugar yogurt

2 ounces shaved chocolate (about ⅓ cup)

Coat an 8-inch pie plate with vegetable oil spray. Sprinkle the plate with the graham crumbs, making sure the bottom and sides are covered. Soften the yogurt in a food processor or by hand. Pour into the prepared pie plate and scatter shaved chocolate on top.

Makes 6 servings

PER SERVING: 191 calories (38 percent from fat), 8.1g fat (3.8 g saturated, 2.2 g monounsaturated), 4 mg cholesterol, 5.5 g protein, 26.3 g carbohydrates, 3.5 g fiber, 123 mg sodium

HELPFUL HINTS

- If chocolate graham crackers are unavailable, use regular graham crackers.

- Select a flavor of low-sugar frozen yogurt that is a family favorite.

- This should be made a day ahead to give the yogurt a chance to refreeze.

Celebration Tea

Graduations, showers, birthdays—here's a delightful way to celebrate. Tea is an easy way to entertain. Everything can be made in advance. Just before the guests arrive, the platters may be placed on the table and the water boiled for the tea. For a celebration, try a champagne toast after the tea and sandwiches have been served, and before the tarts and fruit arrive.

Menu

Tea 244

Smoked Salmon Sandwiches 245

Watercress Sandwiches 246

Cucumber Sandwiches 247

Smoked Ham Sandwiches 248

Fruit Kebabs 249

Lemon Curd Tartlets 249

COUNTDOWN

Two days ahead

- Shop for ingredients.

On the day

- Prepare the recipes.

SHOPPING LIST

Dairy

- 1 small container nonfat ricotta cheese

Deli

- 1 package lean deli ham (¼ pound needed)

Seafood

- 1 package smoked salmon (¼ pound needed)

Grocery

- 1 container tea
- 1 bottle sweet pickle relish
- 1 bottle lemon curd
- 6 small wooden skewers
- 1 package frozen phyllo tart cases (1½ inches in diameter)

Produce

- 1 lemon
- 1 small bunch fresh dill
- 1 bunch watercress
- 1 small bunch mint leaves
- 1 English-style (seedless) cucumber
- 1 honeydew melon
- 1 cantaloupe melon
- 1 bunch seedless grapes
- 1 container fresh pineapple cubes

Staples

- Butter
- Whole wheat bread
- Whole grain bread
- Reduced-fat mayonnaise
- Dijon mustard
- Black peppercorns

The recipes for this party contain 501 calories with 40 percent of calories from fat.

TEA

Following the British time-honored method of making tea produces an excellent result.

To make a proper pot of tea, choose a good-quality tea and keep it in an airtight container in a dry place. Each time tea is made, the kettle should be completely emptied of water and then filled with fresh cold water. Put the water on to boil. While the water is boiling, warm your teapot by filling it with hot water from the faucet and then draining it. Measure 1 teaspoon of tea per cup made, plus one for the pot. As soon as the water boils, pour it onto the leaves. Replace the teapot lid and let the tea steep for 3 to 5 minutes. Stir the tea before it is served. For tea bags, use 1 tea bag per cup following the same method. Place a small tray with milk, lemon slices, and sugar on the table for people to select what they prefer.

SMOKED SALMON SANDWICHES

4 teaspoons butter, softened

4 slices whole wheat bread, thinly sliced

¼ pound smoked salmon

1 tablespoon lemon juice

2 tablespoons fresh dill

Freshly ground black pepper

Butter the slices of bread. Using a knife, spread salmon over each slice, completely covering it. Sprinkle salmon with lemon juice, dill, and a little pepper. Cut diagonally into 4 triangles to make 16 open-faced sandwiches.

Makes 6 servings

PER SERVING: 153 calories (53 percent from fat), 9.1 g fat (3.1 g saturated, 4.3 g monounsaturated), 28 mg cholesterol, 9.4 g protein, 9.3 g carbohydrates, 1.7 g fiber, 257 mg sodium

HELPFUL HINTS FOR ALL TEA SANDWICHES:

- Sandwiches can be made several hours ahead. To keep the sandwiches moist, place them on a serving platter and place a damp (not wet) paper towel over them. Then cover the platter with plastic wrap.

- Make sure the butter is soft enough to evenly spread over the bread.

- Traditional tea sandwiches have the crusts cut off. You can leave the crusts on if you prefer.

WATERCRESS SANDWICHES

1½ cups watercress, large
   stems removed

4 teaspoons butter

4 slices whole wheat
   bread

Chop the watercress. Butter the bread and place watercress on 2 slices. Cover with remaining 2 slices and gently press together. Cut diagonally into triangles to make 8 sandwiches.

Makes 6 servings

PER SERVING: 70 calories (43 percent from fat), 3.4 g fat (1.8 g saturated, 1.1 g monounsaturated), 7 mg cholesterol, 2.0 g protein, 8.7 g carbohydrates, 1.3 g fiber, 128 mg sodium

CUCUMBER SANDWICHES

1 cup sliced cucumber
(seedless English
cucumber, if possible)

2 tablespoons reduced-
fat mayonnaise

4 slices whole wheat
bread, thinly sliced

Peel and thinly slice the cucumber about ⅛ inch thick. Spread mayonnaise on the bread. Completely cover 2 slices with 2 layers of cucumber. Place the remaining bread slices on top and gently press the bread to flatten. Cut into ½-inch thick fingers to make 8 sandwiches.

Makes 6 servings

PER SERVING: 65 calories (34 percent from fat), 2.5 g fat (0.4 g saturated, 0.8 g monounsaturated), 2 mg cholesterol, 2.0 g protein, 9.6 g carbohydrates, 1.4 g fiber, 139 mg sodium

SMOKED HAM SANDWICHES

1 tablespoon Dijon
  mustard

4 slices whole grain
  bread, thinly sliced

2 tablespoons sweet
  pickle relish

¼ pound lean deli ham,
  thinly sliced

Spread mustard over 2 slices of bread. Spread relish over mustard. Place ham over mustard and cover with remaining slices of bread. Press gently to flatten bread. Cut diagonally into triangles to make 8 sandwiches.

Makes 6 servings

PER SERVING: 82 calories (21 percent from fat), 2.0 g fat (0.5 g saturated, 0.9 g monounsaturated), 10 mg cholesterol, 5.9 g protein, 10.8 g carbohydrates, 1.4 g fiber, 390 mg sodium

FRUIT KEBABS

6 cubes honeydew melon
(about 1 cup)

6 cubes cantaloupe
(about 1 cup)

12 red seedless grapes

6 fresh pineapple cubes

6 small wooden skewers

Place 1 honeydew cube, 1 cantaloupe cube, 2 grapes, and 1 pineapple cube on each skewer. Arrange skewers on a serving platter.

Makes 6 servings

PER SERVING: 40 calories (5 percent from fat), 0.2 g fat (0 g saturated, 0 g monounsaturated), 0 mg cholesterol, 0.5 g protein, 10.1 g carbohydrates, 0.9 g fiber, 8 mg sodium

LEMON CURD TARTLETS

6 tablespoons nonfat
ricotta cheese

4 tablespoons lemon
curd

12 phyllo tart cases
(1½ inches in diameter)

6 baby mint leaves

Mix ricotta cheese and lemon curd together until smooth. Fill the tart cases. Place a mint leaf on top.

Makes 6 servings

PER SERVING: 91 calories (50 percent from fat), 5.1 g fat (0.3 g saturated, 0 g monounsaturated), 16 mg cholesterol, 4.0 g protein, 16.1 g carbohydrates, 0.8 g fiber, 57 mg sodium

Mediterranean Dinner

The flavors of Morocco add an intriguing mix to this Mediterranean party. The Turkey Tagine is a Moroccan peasant dish. With its fragrant blend of spices, it's one of the most frequently served dishes in that country.

Menu

Moroccan Turkey Tagine 252

Orange Olive Rice 253

Cucumber and Tomato Salad 254

Lime Cinnamon Sherbet 255

COUNTDOWN

Two days ahead

- Shop for ingredients.
- Make Lime Cinnamon Sherbet.

One day ahead

- Make Moroccan Turkey Tagine.
- Make Orange Olive Rice.

Two hours before guests arrive

- Make Cucumber and Tomato Salad.

30 minutes before guests arrive

- Rewarm tagine and rice in 300-degree oven for 15 minutes, or until warm to the touch.

Just before serving dessert

- Scoop Lime Cinnamon Sherbet into ice cream cones.

SHOPPING LIST

Meat

- 1 package turkey breast (2¼ pounds needed)

Grocery

- 1 container turmeric
- 1 container ground cumin
- 1 package lentils
- 1 jar pitted green olives
- 1 container lime sherbet
- 1 package small wafer, flat-bottom ice cream cones

Produce

- 5 medium tomatoes
- 1 bunch cilantro
- 1 bunch parsley
- 1 bunch mint
- 1 large bag washed, ready-to-eat spinach
- 2 oranges
- 2 lemons
- 1 cucumber
- 1 bunch scallions

Staples

- 10-minute brown rice
- Olive oil
- Onion
- Ground cinnamon
- Salt
- Black peppercorns

HELPFUL HINT

- Tagine also refers to the glazed earthenware dish with a conical lid used for slow cooking the ingredients. Steam gathers in the top of the conical lid and falls on the food, keeping it moist without basting. Any type of skillet or casserole can be used for this dinner.

- This meal tastes even better made a day ahead. The turkey absorbs more of the spice flavors.

MOROCCAN TURKEY TAGINE

3 tablespoons olive oil

3 cups sliced onion

3 medium tomatoes, cut into 8 wedges

1½ teaspoons turmeric

1½ teaspoons ground cinnamon

3 teaspoons ground cumin

Salt and freshly ground black pepper

2 cups water

10 fresh cilantro sprigs plus 2 tablespoons chopped leaves

1 cup dried lentils

12 cups washed, ready-to-eat spinach

2¼ pounds turkey breast meat, cut into bite-size pieces

Heat oil over high heat in a skillet or casserole dish. Add the onion, tomatoes, turmeric, cinnamon, cumin, and salt and black pepper to taste. Cook 2 minutes to release the juices in the dried spices. Add water, cilantro, and lentils. Bring the water to a simmer, reduce heat to medium, cover, and gently simmer 20 minutes. Add more water if casserole becomes dry. Remove cilantro sprigs, stir in spinach and turkey, and cook 3 minutes, or until the turkey is cooked and the spinach wilts. Add salt and pepper to taste.

Makes 6 servings

PER SERVING: 424 calories (20 percent from fat), 9.3 g fat (1.5 g saturated, 5.6 g monounsaturated), 108 mg cholesterol, 53.2 g protein, 33.3 g carbohydrates, 7.6 g fiber, 143 mg sodium

ORANGE OLIVE RICE

1½ cups 10-minute brown rice

3 cups water

2 tablespoons olive oil

1 teaspoon cumin

Salt and freshly ground black pepper

2 oranges, segmented and cut into 1-inch pieces (about 2 cups)

18 pitted green olives, cut in half

½ cup chopped parsley

Place rice and water in a medium saucepan. Bring to a boil, lower heat, and simmer 10 minutes. Drain and place in a serving bowl. Add olive oil, cumin, and salt and pepper to taste. Toss well. Add orange segments and olives and toss well. Scatter parsley on top.

Makes 6 servings

PER SERVING: 258 calories (26 percent from fat), 7.5 g fat (1.1 g saturated, 4.9 g monounsaturated), 0 mg cholesterol, 4.6 g protein, 44.1 g carbohydrates, 3.6 g fiber, 121 mg sodium

HELPFUL HINT

- Any type of quick-cooking rice can be used. Follow package instructions. Count ½ cup cooked rice per person.

CUCUMBER AND TOMATO SALAD

2 tablespoons olive oil

2 tablespoons lemon juice

3 cups coarsely chopped cucumber

2 cups coarsely chopped tomatoes

½ cup sliced scallion

2 tablespoons fresh mint

Salt and freshly ground black pepper

Mix olive oil and lemon juice together in a salad bowl. Add the cucumber, tomatoes, scallion, and mint. Add salt and pepper to taste. Toss well.

Makes 6 servings

PER SERVING: 63 calories (68 percent from fat), 4.7 g fat (0.7 g saturated, 3.4 g monounsaturated), 0 mg cholesterol, 1.4 g protein, 5.0 g carbohydrates, 1.4 g fiber, 6 mg sodium

LIME CINNAMON SHERBET

3 cups lime sherbet

2 teaspoons ground cinnamon

6 small wafer, flat-bottom ice cream cones

Soften sherbet and mix with cinnamon. Place in a container and return to freezer. Just before serving, scoop into 6 cones.

Makes 6 servings

PER SERVING: 149 calories (2 percent from fat), 0.3 g fat (0.1 g saturated, 0.1 g monounsaturated), 0 mg cholesterol, 0.4 g protein, 36.8 g carbohydrates, 1.5 g fiber, 21 mg sodium

HELPFUL HINT

- Any citrus-flavored sherbet can be used.

Housewarming Party

Homemade mushroom soup, French-style roasted chicken, Eggplant Provencal, and Pear Crumble create a bistro dinner that will delight your friends for a housewarming or anytime.

Menu

Mushroom Soup 258

French Herb Chicken 259

Eggplant Provencal 260

Pear Crumble 261

COUNTDOWN

Two days ahead

- Shop for ingredients.

One day ahead

- Make Mushroom Soup.

On the day

- Make French Herb Chicken.
- Make Eggplant Provencal.

Two hours before guests arrive

- Make Pear Crumble.

SHOPPING LIST

Meat

- 1 package skinless chicken thighs (3½ pounds needed)

Grocery

- 1 bottle herbes de Provence
- 1 container ground nutmeg
- 1 small bottle dry white wine
- 2 loaves whole wheat baguettes
- 1 jar low-sodium pasta sauce
- 1 jar pitted black olives
- 1 bottle almond extract

Produce

- 1 pound portobello mushrooms
- 1 pound eggplant
- 4 pears

Staples

- Canola oil
- Olive oil
- Onion
- Garlic
- Flour
- Cornstarch
- Butter
- Sugar
- Olive oil spray
- Fat-free, low-sodium chicken broth
- Salt
- Black peppercorns

The recipes for this party contain 826 calories with 30 percent of calories from fat.

HELPFUL HINTS

- If made a day ahead, taste for seasoning before serving and add more if needed.

- Any type of mushroom can be used.

MUSHROOM SOUP

1 tablespoon canola oil

3 cups sliced onion

1 pound portobello mushrooms, washed and sliced

1 tablespoon flour

24 ounces fat-free, low-sodium chicken broth

¼ teaspoon ground nutmeg

Salt and freshly ground black pepper

Heat oil in a large saucepan. Add onion and cook until golden, about 5 minutes. Add mushrooms. Sprinkle flour on top and stir until absorbed. Add broth and bring to a boil. Lower heat and gently simmer for 20 minutes. Add nutmeg and salt and pepper to taste, and check the seasoning. Add more nutmeg if needed.

Makes 6 servings

PER SERVING: 86 calories (27 percent from fat), 2.6 g fat (0.4 g saturated, 1.7 g monounsaturated), 0 mg cholesterol, 4.6 g protein, 12.8 g carbohydrates, 2.0 g fiber, 291 mg sodium

FRENCH HERB CHICKEN

3½ pounds skinless
chicken thighs, with
bone

½ teaspoon salt or to
taste

2 cloves garlic, crushed
Olive oil spray

2 tablespoons herbes
de Provence

1 cup + 2 tablespoons
fat-free, low-sodium
chicken broth

1 tablespoon cornstarch

1 cup dry white wine

2 loaves whole wheat
baguettes

Preheat oven to 400 degrees. Place chicken in a roasting pan and sprinkle with salt. Rub garlic into chicken. Spray chicken with olive oil spray and sprinkle with herbes de Provence. Pour 1 cup chicken broth around chicken thighs. Place chicken in oven and bake 30 minutes. A meat thermometer should read 180 degrees.

Remove chicken to a serving platter and pour the pan juices into a saucepan. Add the wine, bring to a boil and reduce by one third, 3 to 4 minutes. Mix the remaining 2 tablespoons chicken broth with the cornstarch and add to the saucepan. Bring to a boil to thicken sauce. Spoon sauce over chicken. Serve with sliced baguettes.

Makes 6 servings

PER SERVING: 460 calories (20 percent from fat), 10.3 g fat (2.3 g saturated, 2.8 g monounsaturated), 138 mg cholesterol, 41.7 g protein, 42.1 g carbohydrates, 3.6 g fiber, 614 mg sodium

HELPFUL HINTS

- Herbes de Provence is a mixture of herbs made in the south of France. It can be found in the spice section of many markets. If unavailable, mix 2 teaspoons each of dried ground rosemary, sage, and thyme.

- Skinless chicken thighs with the bone can be found in the meat section of the super-market.

- To rewarm chicken, cover with foil and place in a 300-degree oven for 15 minutes, or until warm to the touch.

- This can be served hot or cold or rewarmed. To rewarm, place in a 300-degree oven for 15 minutes. Sprinkle parsley on just before serving.

- Salting the eggplant removes the bitter liquids from the eggplant and prevents it from absorbing too much oil during cooking. Be sure to rinse the salt off and dry with a paper towel before cooking.

- For even slices, look for a long, straight eggplant, if possible.

- Divide the oil in half and use two nonstick skillets to cook eggplant.

EGGPLANT PROVENCAL

1 pound eggplant
  Salt
¼ cup flour
3 tablespoons olive oil
¾ cup low-sodium pasta sauce
12 pitted black olives
¼ cup chopped parsley (optional)

Wash eggplant and trim on either end, leaving skin on. Cut into 12 round slices about ½ inch thick. Sprinkle slices with salt and score on each side with a fork. Place the slices on a baking tray and place another tray on top. Leave for 30 minutes.

Preheat oven to 325 degrees. Rinse the salt from the eggplant and pat dry with a paper towel. Dip the slices into the flour. Heat the oil in a large nonstick skillet and lightly brown the slices on each side. Drain on a paper towel. Place on a baking sheet and put in the oven for 10 minutes.

Warm the pasta sauce in a saucepan or microwave oven. Spread some on each eggplant slice. Cut the olives in half and place 2 halves in the center of each slice. Sprinkle parsley on top, if desired.

Makes 6 servings

PER SERVING: 115 calories (62 percent from fat), 7.9 g fat (1.1 g saturated, 5.7 g monounsaturated), 0 mg cholesterol, 1.9 g protein, 10.4 g carbohydrates, 3.3 g fiber, 84 mg sodium

PEAR CRUMBLE

4 ripe pears, peeled and
   sliced
2 teaspoons almond
   extract
6 tablespoons flour
2 tablespoons sugar
3 tablespoons butter

Toss pear slices with almond extract. Microwave pears in individual ramekins for 2 minutes or poach in water for 2 minutes, or until soft. Mix flour and sugar together. Cut in butter and rub with fingertips to make a crumbly texture. Spoon over pears. Place under broiler for 5 minutes, or until topping is golden.

Makes 6 servings

PER SERVING: 165 calories (34 percent from fat), 6.3 g fat (3.6 g saturated, 1.7 g monounsaturated), 16 mg cholesterol, 1.3 g protein, 27.0 g carbohydrates, 3.0 g fiber, 59 mg sodium

HELPFUL HINT

- Make sure butter is very cold.

INDEX

Boldfaced page references indicate photographs.